C902294678

"Cynthia Kim unequivocally captures the true essence of what it means to be autistic! What it means to be me! She helps you understand yourself, which enables you to struggle less with yourself and life. There's no doubt about it that Aspies are complex. Kim addresses all facets of what makes us different head-on. From shutting down to contentment and peace, it's all covered in this eye-opening account of living with Asperger's. Insight and advice follow each section for a clear and concise plan to help in your everyday life."

—Anita Lesko, BSN, RN, MS, CRNA, internationally recognized autism advocate and author of Been There. Done That. Try This!, *also published by Jessica Kingsley Publishers*

"In this honest and beautifully articulate book, Cynthia Kim reflects back on her life before and after her recent diagnosis, and she describes how her diagnosis helped her to gain a new understanding of herself and events in her past. The book is packed full of useful tips for others with Asperger's, and her own experiences with marriage and raising a child provide a valuable perspective that is both eye-opening and a real pleasure to read."

—Elisabeth Hurley, PhD, Research Officer, Autism West Midlands, UK

"I have been a fan of Cynthia Kim's blog, *Musings of an Aspie*, for many years. This book has everything I've come to expect from her blog and more. Poignant and practical by turns, and always insightful, this book is a must-read for anyone trying to get a better understanding of autism."

—Lynne Soraya, blogger for Psychology Today *and author of* Living Independently on the Autism Spectrum

of related interest

Pretending to be Normal
Living with Asperger's Syndrome (Autism Spectrum Disorder)
2nd Edition
Liane Holliday Willey
ISBN 978 1 84905 755 4
eISBN 978 0 85700 987 6

Aspergirls
Empowering Females with Asperger Syndrome
Rudy Simone
Foreword by Liane Holliday Willey
ISBN 978 1 84905 826 1
eISBN 978 0 85700 289 1

Been There. Done That. Try This!
An Aspie's Guide to Life on Earth
Edited by Tony Attwood, Craig R. Evans and Anita Lesko
ISBN 978 1 84905 964 0
eISBN 978 0 85700 871 8

To Sang Hwan,
who has embraced
every step of this journey

Contents

Acknowledgments

This book began as me talking to myself, posting entries to a brand new blog that no one was reading. I saw it as free therapy, a way to process my feelings about discovering that I was autistic. As I found other bloggers and began to participate in the online autism community, a group of writers took me under their wing and shared my blog posts with their readers. In particular, I want to thank my fellow bloggers Ariane Zurcher, Heather Clark, Leah Kelley, and Shawna Hinkle. I am deeply grateful for their encouragement and support in those early days.

I have been fortunate to be blessed with an active and enthusiastic group of people who comment on my blog, sharing their stories and experiences. While they are too numerous to mention by name, I am sincerely grateful to each and every one of them. They have enriched my writing by helping me better understand what it means to be autistic and by keeping me honest. Time and again, I'm reminded of how much those on the spectrum have in common and at the same time how varied we are. I am especially indebted to Kathryn Black, Anne Dane, and Nat Titman for their extensive feedback on early drafts of much of what eventually made it into this book.

Thank you to the editors who have published my work over the past two years, including Julia Begley and Elisabeth Hurley at Autism West Midlands, Shannon Des Roches Rosa at *Thinking Person's Guide to Autism*, Leslie Burby at *Autism Parenting Magazine*, and Sharon da Vanport at Autism Women's Network.

I owe special thanks to Ariane Zurcher for inadvertently inspiring the structure of this book. Her chance comment in an online discussion helped me find the thread that would bind all of the pieces together.

It's not an exaggeration to say that Jessica Kingsley has made one of my long-time dreams come true by bringing this book into print. I am indebted to her and to the people at Jessica Kingsley Publishers, particularly Bethany Gower, Victoria Peters, and Lisa Clark, who have been a pleasure to work with.

Over the past two years, I've been privileged to meet many, many dedicated bloggers and advocates who are working tirelessly to promote autism acceptance. The sense of community I've found among them has been a source of joy and strength. Thank you especially to Sarah Ackermann, Etienne Anders, Emily Paige Ballou, Heather Clark, Sharon da Vanport, Anne Dane, Jeannie Davide Rivera, Lori Miller Degtiarev, Adrienne Erazo, Alex Forshaw, Alyssa Hillary, Shawna Hinkle, Natalie Genz Jerkins, Sparrow Rose Jones, Leah Kelley, Sandy Kinnamon, Ine Louw, Michael Scott Monje Jr., Beth Ryan, Kassiane Alexandra Sibley, Renee Salas, Amy Sequenzia, Linda Stanley, Nat Titman, Lei Wiley-Mydske, and Ariane Zurcher.

In spite of my best efforts, I'm sure there are people I've forgotten to include here and I beg their forgiveness.

I am grateful to my parents Bill and Judy, who gave me the space to be me when I was growing up and who indulged all of my many childhood obsessions.

Special thanks and love to my daughter Jess. Not only has she been my number one cheerleader on this project from day one, she has generously allowed me to write about our relationship and has unflinchingly shared her thoughts about what it means to have an autistic mom. Her insight and support have been invaluable throughout the writing of this book and always.

Most of all, thank you to Sang, for being there, always. Throughout the writing of this book, he read my drafts, made suggestions, pushed me to dig deeper, gamely played along with my experiments, and listened to me ramble about autism in the way only someone with a newly discovered special interest can. More than that, he has been my constant in life, there to lift me up when I'm feeling down and to catch me when I fall and, most of all, to fly beside me when I soar.

1

Nerdy, Shy, and Socially Inappropriate

I've been autistic all my life, but I didn't know it until I was in my forties.

I grew up in an era when my diagnosis—Asperger's Syndrome—didn't yet exist. Kids like me were labeled nerdy, shy, or gifted. Year after year I brought home report cards that said I didn't work and play well with others, didn't participate in class.

Because I was quiet and did well academically, the adults in my life attributed my difficulties to extreme shyness and timidity. I'd grow out of it eventually and all of my problems would be solved. That explanation carried me into adulthood, where in the back of my mind I was waiting to magically outgrow my social and communication difficulties.

Like a lot of autistic adults of my generation, I made it well into middle age before realizing that I wasn't just shy or weird or nerdy. That I wasn't going to outgrow my quirks and wake up one day to suddenly find I was "normal."

No matter how hard I tried—and believe me I never stopped trying—I found it impossible to master fundamental people skills. Making friends, mingling at parties, mixing in with the other moms at PTA meetings, the simplest social interactions remained a mystery to me. No longer a child, I couldn't continue to hide out on the fringes of social groups.

I had a daughter of my own to raise and a business to run, a marriage to hold together. Somehow I made it all work, though it was obvious to me that something was not quite right. Shyness is cute in a five-year-old girl; in a 30-year-old woman, not so much.

Decades passed and there I was, still waiting for someone to give me the secret handbook that would explain all those social nuances the people around me seemed to instinctivelygrasp.

To my surprise, what I got instead was an autism spectrum diagnosis. It was shocking at first, to learn that I'd lived more than 40 years of my life not knowing something so fundamental and important about myself. For the first few months after learning about Asperger's I spent a lot of time playing "What if…?"

What if I'd been diagnosed earlier? What if I'd been given the type of supports and accommodations that children on the spectrum receive today? Of course, it's impossible to know how my life would have been different.

On the face of it, I'm a typical suburban middle-aged woman. I'm happily married, a successful small business owner, and proud mom to a terrific young woman. Someone might look at those outward signs of success and wonder whether I'm really *that* autistic.

Spend a day or even a few hours with me, and you'll stop wondering. I have all of the telltale signs of Asperger's: poor social skills, communication difficulties, sensory sensitivities, a deep love of routines, lots of subtle stims, the working memory of a goldfish…the list is long and varied.

Playing Life in "Hard Mode"

Growing up undiagnosed forced me to make a lot of adaptations instinctively. I'd learned how to work around, minimize and accommodate many of the traits that make life on the spectrum challenging. Still, I often felt like I was playing life in "hard mode."

Deciding to finally attend college in my late 30s forced me to face just how much effort I put into working around, minimizing and accommodating what I thought of as quirks.

My job is a perfect example. I've been my own boss since I was 19, which has allowed me to decide who I work with and how. That resulted in some rather unusual ideas about socially acceptable workplace behavior. Walking around the office in my socks? Yes! Bringing my dog to work? Why not? Eating lunch in my office with the door closed? Essential.

By ensuring that I was the one making the rules, I wrapped myself in a cocoon of relative safety. If I didn't want to do something, I delegated it, hired someone to do it, or avoided it.

Taking classes at a university forced me to follow someone else's rules if I wanted to succeed. I was judged on not only my academic work but my communication skills. My thinking process was subject to scrutiny. I had to make oral presentations and work in teams. There was no locked door to hide behind while I ate lunch.

That was a lot to put up with. On the other hand, I really wanted to earn my degree, to prove that I might be a little late, but I could make it through college.

I did my best to fit in where I could. When things got rough, I sucked it up and muddled through, telling myself that as a "returning student" most of the young people in my class were going to look at me funny anyhow.

It's hard to say exactly when I went from thinking, "I'm a little odd" to "Maybe there's something systemically different about me." The process was a lot like putting together a puzzle—connecting pieces here and there, assembling bits of the scene but not being able to see the whole picture until dozens of those little connections were made.

A few of the key pieces:

- The sociology class assignment that asked me to describe a time when someone's body language didn't match their words. My initial response: "What body language?" When we shared our answers in class, I discovered how unusual it is to not instinctively notice body language.

- The way professors so often asked me if I had a question or looked directly at me while asking, "Is everyone following what I'm saying?" I didn't know it at the time, but I often frown—typically a sign of confusion—when I'm concentrating.

- The universal look of surprise I got from professors after the first test or paper was graded. I rarely speak in class and when I do, it's a crapshoot whether I'll completely misinterpret a question, give an off-the-wall response or get the right answer. But write a 30-page paper about the economic impacts of environmental regulation? Yeah, I'm all over that.

It wasn't until I came across a radio story on Asperger's Syndrome during my final year of school that the puzzle pieces started to reveal the bigger picture. While I'd heard of Asperger's, I'd never considered that it might be something that applied to me. Sure I could see myself in some of the symptoms, but who didn't?

I'd told myself that having Asperger's was similar to being shy—a really bad case of shyness—which made it easy to dismiss. And I wasn't *that* shy, was I? I had a job, a child, a husband. I interacted with people when necessary.

I carefully avoided the qualifiers. I had a job that I'd structured around all of my little neuroses. I had a child to whom I'd stopped saying the words "I love you" as soon as she was old enough to talk. I had a husband who was growing increasingly frustrated with my often cold, controlling behavior. I interacted with people *when necessary* and no more.

There was an element of good fortune that allowed me to get away with all of the hacks and workarounds I'd devised to compensate for my deficits. Through a combination of luck and a willingness to take risks that a lot people wouldn't, I'd managed to create an environment that capitalized on what I could do and masked most of the things I couldn't.

Being in school upset the delicate balance I'd worked so hard to cobble together. Suddenly it had become hard to avoid the qualifiers.

As I listened to the radio story on Asperger's, I felt like they were talking about me. Not about someone *like* me, but about *me*. I don't know what made that story different from the others I'd come across about Asperger's. And there had been many—my fascination with Asperger's Syndrome and autism should have been an obvious red flag, warning me that my subconscious was trying to tell me something.

Maybe I was finally ready to see the big picture. I'd certainly assembled enough of the little clusters of puzzle pieces to make it possible. Whatever the cause, the result was a feeling of lightness—like Asperger's Syndrome was a bucket that would hold all of the things about myself that I found confusing and painful and shameful and frustrating and hard. Maybe finally having a place to put all those things would mean I wouldn't have to juggle them anymore.

Intrigued, I began reading everything I could find about autism spectrum conditions. It quickly became obvious that Asperger's was more than a collection of social and communication problems.

There were dozens of little tells that were undeniably me and had nothing to do with being shy or introverted. The way I often talk too loudly or too quietly. The intense interests in unusual topics. My blunt honesty. My heavy dependence on lists and routines. The way I don't recognize people "out of context." My discomfort with compliments. The list was long enough for me to finally admit that it might be a good idea to get evaluated for an autism spectrum condition.

As hard as that admission was, once it became clear that I was likely on the autism spectrum, my first reaction was relief. It explained so much about my life that I'd thought was my fault—for not trying hard enough or being good enough. It wasn't an excuse but it was a hell of a good explanation.

As I learned more about Asperger's and about myself, the initial relief gave way to a rollercoaster of emotions: anger, grief, resentment, fear, surprise, confusion, acceptance, joy, optimism and increasingly a deep, liberating sense of peace.

I finally had the right context for the labels I'd carried with me all my life, the ones that never quite felt like a complete explanation: *nerdy, shy, socially inappropriate*. Yes, I was the bookish, nerdy kid. The quirky teenager who loved karate and knew far too many random facts. I was always the quiet one, too shy to speak up in class, too introverted to chase after boys or go to parties. I was the kid with the weird friends and the weirder habits.

That shy, nerdy little girl grew up, but little changed. Soon she was the woman who didn't seem to notice that it was socially inappropriate to wear the same clothes every day. The woman who knew even more random facts and considered them fascinating dinner party conversation. The woman who still occasionally forgets to check if she's brushed her hair before leaving the house.

Nerdy, shy and socially inappropriate. Those words have followed me since childhood and now I know why. And it's the *why* that has fascinated me. The *why* is what this book is about.

Since discovering that I'm on the spectrum, I've been blogging about my experiences, processing what it means to suddenly be autistic at 42. In a way, I've been forced to relearn how to be me. All the things that I thought were broken or defective or weird about me? It turns out they're perfectly normal for people like me. Even more exciting? There actually *are* other people like me. Lots of them.

As I've gotten to know other autistic adults, I've come to realize that we have much in common and we are as diverse as any other group of people. There are few traits that are universal, which makes it hard to write a definitive book about life on the spectrum.

What I've written instead is what the experience of being—and of becoming—autistic has meant for me. There has been much to discover—about autism, about disability, about compassion and community and self. I have spent hundreds of hours reading and researching, measuring theory and practice against my own experience. It's not an exaggeration to say that "all things autism" has become my new special interest.

The process of writing this book, of unpacking the hard and sad and joyful aspects of my life in the context of Asperger's, has changed me more than any other experience in my life.

Nerdy, shy and socially inappropriate are no longer labels for me to shrink away from or offer up apologetically as an explanation for yet another awkward social encounter. I'm proud to be a nerd, I've traded in shy for the more neutral-sounding quiet and I'm unapologetically socially inappropriate. Understanding Asperger's has helped me understand myself and that's made all the difference.

2

Growing up Undiagnosed

One of the first questions that arose after my initial realization that I might be autistic was: "How could no one have noticed?" Growing up, I was definitely different from my peers. For one thing, I spent hours alone. Some of my happiest memories are of long bike rides around my rural neighborhood, exploring in the woods, and playing games in my room, all by myself. I remember quite a few fiercely contested games of *Risk* and *Monopoly* that pitted me against myself.

My parents never questioned what I did for hours in my room with the door closed. If I disappeared for the afternoon into the woods behind our house, their only concern was that I be home by five-thirty for dinner.

I don't know what would have happened if I came home at six. I was a good girl and good girls followed the rules.

The problem with being the good girl, especially if you're a young undiagnosed Aspie, is that good girls are invisible. Boys on the spectrum tend to act out. They're more likely to have problems with anger management or to be labeled defiant and oppositional. They're less likely to be team players, shrinking away from competition and refusing to follow the rules.

Years ago these boys got slapped with labels like "juvenile delinquent" and "behavior problem" while girls like me got labeled "painfully shy" or "awkward." There was no such thing as an Asperger's Syndrome diagnosis for children in the 1960s, 70s or 80s. Those who were diagnosed with autism tended to be nonverbal or late to acquire language.

This is one of the main reasons that so many adults are now being diagnosed with an autism spectrum disorder (ASD) in their thirties, forties, fifties, or later. Women in particular seem to have escaped diagnosis, even as their brothers were diagnosed in childhood with ASD.

Gender Differences

Today, out of every ten children diagnosed with ASD, eight will be boys and two will be girls. The big question raised by this disparity is: are boys more likely to be autistic or are they just more likely to get diagnosed because their symptoms tend to fit the classic manifestation of ASD?

Both Leo Kanner, the researcher who originally identified the traits of autism in 1943, and Hans Asperger, who first identified the traits of Asperger's syndrome in 1944, based their definitions primarily on studies of boys. Kanner's definition of autism forms the basis of the ASD diagnostic criteria still in use: deficits in social interaction and language as well as the presence of stereotyped and repetitive behaviors.

Similarly, Asperger's criteria were used to diagnose the condition that bears his name between 1994 when it became a formal diagnosis and 2013 when it was subsumed under the broader category of autism sprectrum disorder in the American Psychiatric Association's revised *Diagnostic and Statistical Manual of Mental Disorders* (DSM-5). Asperger concluded that although they had average or above-average intelligence, the boys in his study had poor nonverbal communication skills, failed to show empathy with their peers, spoke in an overly formal way, were clumsy and were drawn toward all-absorbing interests that dominated their conversations.

Increasingly, experts are realizing that ASD looks different in girls than it does in boys, perhaps accounting for the lower rate at which girls and women are diagnosed. For example, boys are more likely to have a special interest in something mechanical—like trains, engines, or elevators—usually at a level far more intense than is age-appropriate. I read a case study about a teenage boy who was obsessed with cataloging the different types of outhouses found in his region. And recently, on a tour of Washington, DC I sat behind a boy who knew more about the history of U.S. presidents than the tour guide. This kind of deep, obscure knowledge is an obvious tipoff that a child is a little different.

Girls, however, are more likely to develop a special interest in something that doesn't stand out quite so much, like music groups, television shows, or fictional characters or worlds. A five-year-old girl who collects Barbies or a ten-year-old girl obsessed with Narnia may not seem that unusual until you look more closely.

As a kid, I collected a lot of things: coins, stamps, baseball cards. I loved to organize my collections and was thrilled when I discovered a new addition at a coin show or in my monthly stamp club delivery. These were somewhat unusual hobbies for a girl my age, but I also played with Barbies, collected dolls, loved to sew my own clothes and voraciously read *Nancy Drew* mysteries.

Anyone who looked closely enough would have noticed that I spent more time organizing and categorizing my Barbies and their clothing than actually playing with them. That my *Nancy Drew* mysteries were lined up on my shelf in numerical order. And all of those clothes I spent hours sewing? I rarely wore them. I mostly liked the process of cutting out the patterns and putting everything together like a big cloth puzzle.

The signs were there, but they were far more subtle than those being given off by the little boy who can identify every

World War II fighter plane or wants his dad to drive him all over the state photographing outhouses.

Social expectations may contribute to the underdiagnosis of girls. It's socially acceptable (or even desirable) for a girl to be shy or quiet. The same passive tendencies in a boy are perceived as lack of assertiveness, an unacceptable trait for males in our society.

Throughout childhood I heard that phrase over and over again. "She's just shy." That excused everything. If I didn't participate in discussions in school, it was because I was shy. If I sat on the sidelines at a birthday party or went off to read in an empty bedroom at a family party, it was because I was shy. If I didn't want to be in the school play or I didn't have many friends—all part of my shyness.

I was a good girl. I didn't make waves. What was the problem?

Autistic boys are more likely than autistic girls to act out, which *is* a problem. And autistic boys seem to be less adept than autistic girls at learning to mimic social behaviors. Perhaps this has something to do with the nature of how girls and boys typically play.

Aspies at Play

As young girls, my friends and I often played "school" or "house," cooperative role-playing games in which we acted out scenarios like math class or making dinner. As long as I got to be the teacher or the mother, I loved these games. They played into my need for control and my love of organizing.

If I didn't get to be the teacher or the mother, the game usually ended in a nasty fight between me and the girl who got that role. Other kids' rules made no sense to me. They felt all wrong. I had to be in charge or I wasn't playing. Dr. Tony

Attwood describes this as "god mode"—the way that autistic kids need to control every aspect of a social situation to make it safe for them to interact.

For whatever reason, a few friends tolerated my god mode and hung around, though not all the time. I remember sometimes daily shouting matches that left me without a playmate for the rest of the day.

Unlike boys' games, where there tend to be winners and losers, girls' games are often based on how well a girl cooperates with the group to create an enjoyable role-playing scenario. Boys' games are often competitive—from sports to video games—and the incentive to play lies in the possibility of winning. A boy can often fit in by being good at a skill. If he can get to level ten on a popular video game or has a good jump shot, he'll find other kids to pursue his interests with. For a boy, a specialized skill that's valued by peers may allow him to get by without learning the nuances of building and maintaining friendships.

This may also be why older autistic boys tend to excel at a practical skill, like building computers, writing software code, drawing Manga or solving complex math problems. Even in the absence of excellent social skills, this kind of practical knowledge can give them a foot in the door with a peer group.

From their earliest social interactions, autistic girls have more innate incentives to learn social skills—or at least learn to fake them. This may be another reason why it's easier for girls on the spectrum to stay under the radar as they make their way through the school system and into adolescence. Their social survival depends on it. Perhaps it's the girls who fail to adapt who are most easily diagnosed. Their lack of social skills often results in the sort of isolation, bullying and depression that set off alarm bells in parents and teachers.

Confessions of a Mean Girl

Being teased and bullied is a painful reality for many young (and some not so young) people on the spectrum. Even those of us who had a small group of friends were often subjected to bullying by kids who sensed we were easy victims.

Like many autistic adults, I could fill pages with painful, humiliating memories of being bullied. There was the time in first grade when I offered to share my kickball with some neighborhood kids. They gave it to the big dog who lived across the street and laughed when he ripped it apart. A few years later, the kids at the swim club flushed my favorite t-shirt down the toilet. It had my name on the back in sparkly letters, so when it was fished out of the clogged plumbing everyone knew exactly who it belonged to. In sixth grade, the biggest smelliest boy in the class trapped me in the coat room and kissed me. It was nothing like I imagined my first kiss would be.

Each time, I took what the bullies doled out and told no one. Like a lot of kids who are bullied, I assumed that I had done something to bring it on myself. If it was my fault, I figured it was up to me to fix it.

My solution: becoming a bully. It didn't happen overnight and it certainly wasn't like I woke up one day and thought, "I'm going to torment other kids." It wasn't fun or gratifying. It was an act of self-preservation.

When you're autistic, especially a young undiagnosed autistic left to fend for yourself, school takes on a survivalist aspect. You're the antelope and the bullies are a pack of hungry lions. That may sound dramatic, but when you're a kid who has little idea how social group dynamics work, it's easy to feel like the whole world is out to get you.

For years I put up with the bullying because I didn't know how to stop it. It never occurred to me to tell an adult or ask for help. Autistic kids aren't very good at asking for help. On top of that, I was a little perfectionist. Keeping quiet seemed easier than calling attention to my failure to stop the bullies. Because that's what it felt like to me: a failure. When I looked around, I saw lots of kids who weren't getting bullied. I didn't know what magical attribute allowed them to skate through life without being tormented. I knew I didn't have that ability and I blamed myself for not knowing how to get it.

So I kept trying to figure it out and the bullying continued, on and off, through elementary school. I had a small group of friends in school, which granted me some immunity, but the playground, the bus stop, the walk home from school and playing in my neighborhood were often sources of looming fear.

After that big stinky boy kissed me in sixth grade, he told some other boys that he was going to make me his girlfriend. When one of the boys ominously repeated this to me, I had no idea what it meant. It definitely sounded bad from the way he said it. I could tell by the way he laughed at my stuttering response that he enjoyed seeing how scared and confused I was.

For the rest of the school year, I made sure that I never went in the coatroom alone. I waited—often hiding out in the girls' bathroom—until I was certain the stinky boy had left to walk home before I started to walk along the same route. I watched my back and spent that spring living in fear. The school year ended uneventfully. Looking back, I think he forgot all about his idea of making me his girlfriend. But at the time, it felt like a very real and scary threat.

At some point during that year, I started to realize that there was an alternative to being afraid all the time. Or maybe being afraid all the time made me desperate. Whatever the cause, one day, when one of the mean girls in the neighborhood said something nasty to me, I said something nasty right back.

It felt good. Maybe too good. And it worked. After a few nasty exchanges, she not only stopped bothering me, we became something like friends.

That's how a bully is born.

Soon, instead of just saying mean stuff back to the kids who teased me, I was the one doing the teasing. I found frenemies—developing relationships with other girls that thrived on getting along one day and cutting each other to shreds with insults the next. Soon, all of my friends were other mean girls.

When we got bored with harassing each other, we went looking for easy targets. If you've ever wondered how a bully recognizes an easy target, I'll let you in on a secret. She looks for the kids who are just like she used to be. Kids who are loners and outcasts, afraid to fight back, too shy to stick up for themselves. Kids who stand out because of their looks. Kids who don't have allies to defend them.

It's easy to spot a victim when you've been one yourself.

Within the first few weeks of seventh grade, I found myself sitting across from the principal, a grave-looking old nun who told me that if I didn't shape up, I'd be kicked out of school. I was shocked. Didn't she know I was a good girl? My self-concept hadn't quite caught up with my behavior. In my mind I was still the shy little brainiac who got picked on all the time.

The principal also told me that every time I pointed one finger at someone else, I was pointing three fingers back at myself. I found this fascinating from a kinesiological point of view but had no idea that she was making a metaphorical point. Kids with Asperger's don't do metaphor.

What I did learn that day was not to pick on kids in my grade who had older cousins that would go to the principal. Using patterns to figure out social rules was already one of my specialties. Sometimes the rules I came up with were the opposite of the ones I was supposed to be learning.

Seventh and eighth grades turned out to be one long battle. I was constantly involved in arguments and confrontations. I ruthlessly made fun of weaker kids. If someone else was the butt of the joke, I made sure I was seen laughing at them.

I had become a mean girl.

Why? If I knew how painful it was to be bullied and teased, why was I inflicting it on other kids? I'm not sure I could have explained it at the time. As an adult, I can look back and see that if I got everyone to laugh at another "weird" kid, they weren't laughing at me. If I made another "dorky" kid the center of attention, for a few minutes I was free from worrying about what everyone was thinking about me.

I'd like to say something happened to make me realize how hurtful my behavior was or some wise adult took me aside and set me straight, but my life as a bully ended more gradually. As time went by, being mean felt less and less good. I started to hate the mean girl I'd become. Being mean became painful and exhausting.

In high school, I found interests I could pursue together with people who didn't tease me. The other mean girls drifted away one by one. I had fewer friends, just one close friend, but I wasn't so afraid. I no longer needed to wrap myself in the armor of bullying to get through the school day or walk through my neighborhood.

Am I making excuses for my behavior? No. I was a mean girl and maybe the best thing that old nun could have done was suspend or expel me from the school. That would have been a wake-up call at least. Instead I drifted through three more years of tormenting other kids.

Am I blaming Asperger's Syndrome for my bullying behavior? No. I was smart enough to know that what I was doing was wrong, even if my Asperger's Syndrome prevented me from grasping all of the ramifications.

Am I sorry? Of course I am.

I'm sorry that I made life miserable for other kids who were just doing their best to get through the day. I'm sorry that no one ever stepped in and stopped me. I'm sorry that I didn't know I had other options.

After learning about how autism impacts social communication, I have a better understanding of both why I was bullied and why I resorted to bullying other kids in the absence of better coping strategies.

TRAITS THAT MAKE AUTISTIC INDIVIDUALS VULNERABLE TO BULLYING

- We have trouble reading social cues, especially the cues that tell us when someone is saying one thing but means another.
- We have trouble reading the facial expressions and body language that should be telling us, "Danger, this person intends to harm you."
- We're easy marks for "practical jokes" because we tend to be literal-minded.
- We've often been socialized out of saying "No" even when we're uncomfortable with something.
- We may not have the language abilities to stand up for ourselves under duress.
- We often don't have a group of friends to shelter, defend or stand up for us.
- We tend to care less about social conventions than other people so we make easy targets for mockery based on what's socially "in" or popular.
- We can be easy to provoke, making us a reactive target.
- We may be more likely than others to believe that we've brought harassment on ourselves due to low self-esteem or being conditioned to think we're weird, defective or damaged.

A Different Kind of Label

Given the difficulties of growing up undiagnosed, it would be easy to get lost in regrets. In the wake of my diagnosis, I found myself going through a mourning period. How would my life have been different if I'd been diagnosed in childhood?

Then I realized that, in a way, I had been.

In sixth grade, I was selected for the newly implemented TAG program at my school. TAG stood for Talented and Gifted—a town-wide pilot program that accepted a few sixth graders from each of the elementary schools in our small suburb. On Friday, I got to leave my regular classroom and walk down the hall to the TAG classroom.

Ten geeks, seven of whom were boys. Ten kids who happily pored over reference books on Blitzkrieg and backgammon while the rest of the town's sixth graders were wrestling with the math and reading curriculum we'd finished a year or more ago.

Looking back, in addition to being gifted, most of us were probably on the spectrum as well. We were all socially awkward to some degree. None of us had to be asked twice to choose a topic for our independent research projects. We came to class lugging backpacks filled with resources. We had entire libraries at home on the subjects we wanted to explore.

No matter what we asked to study, Mr. Marek, the aging hippie who taught the class, encouraged us. When I told him I wanted to "study" *MAD* magazine for my second project, he explained the concept of satire and helped me work out *why* the comics were funny.

TAG was Aspie heaven. If I spent the afternoon curled up in a beanbag with my stack of *MAD* magazines, no one told me to return to my seat. If I was the only kid in the class who brought a bag lunch because I couldn't stomach the school pizza, no one at the lunch table made fun of me. If I needed to have a joke explained, even a whole magazine full of them, there was Mr. Marek, ready to patiently answer questions with humor and honesty and not an ounce of condescension.

He thought we were the coolest kids around and, in that classroom, we thought we were too. TAG was my first hint of what it meant to have a tribe of my own.

DOUBLY EXCEPTIONAL

Today, kids like the ones I shared the TAG classroom with are labeled doubly exceptional or twice exceptional. Back then we were the geeks and the nerds. Particularly if you were a girl and you were smart, people seemed to expect you to be weird. "Normal" girls weren't smart and smart girls were quirky.

Adults wrote off our quirks as a byproduct of our intelligence. They sent us out to the playground, assuming we would figure out how to navigate the social minefields that lurked within kickball games and jump rope circles. We were smart. We would get it eventually. When we didn't, they reminded themselves that we were smart and because we were smart, we would get by.

And we did, but not always in the way they hoped we would. Some of us became mean girls. Some of us became depressed or developed eating disorders. Many of us carried those scars from the playground deep into adulthood.

As the concept of giftedness evolved, some theorists put forth the idea of giftedness as asynchronous development, suggesting that gifted children reach intellectual milestones faster than other children but lag in cognitive, social, and emotional development. Proponents of this theory say that children who are hyperlexic, for example, develop in a fundamentally different way because they have access to advanced ideas at an earlier age than other children.

While this may be true of some gifted children, for many it shifts the focus away from their developmental disability—

explaining it away as a byproduct of giftedness. It's easy to look at this model and assume that these children will just magically catch up with their peers developmentally. After all, they're smarter than their peers. What's keeping them from being just as adept in the social and emotional realms?

This is like throwing a child baseball star in the pool, then being surprised if he sinks like a rock. "What do you mean he can't swim? If he's athletic enough to hit a baseball, surely he's athletic enough to swim."

Does a metaphor of a drowning child seem extreme?

If you spent your recesses and bus rides and summers at camp getting mercilessly bullied, physically threatened or worse, you probably don't think so. For kids who are developmentally disabled but intellectually gifted, expecting them to get by on intelligence alone is the equivalent of throwing them in the deep end of the pool without teaching them to swim first. It's leaving them to drown—emotionally and mentally—all the while telling them how smart they are.

WHEN A STRENGTH ISN'T A STRENGTH

Not that encouraging intellectual strengths is a bad thing. Unlike children labeled developmentally disabled and given a deficit-based course of therapy designed to fix them, doubly exceptional children have an advantage in their intelligence.

Unfortunately, part of this advantage is that we can mask a big portion of our disability with coping strategies and adaptations. And when we fail to hide something, people assume we're not trying hard enough. Or we're being deliberately obstinate. Or that we're lazy, defiant, insolent, shy, ditzy, or scatterbrained.

"What's wrong with you?" they ask incredulously. "You can memorize the batting averages of the entire Major League, but you can't remember to put your homework in your backpack?"

The doubly exceptional child grows up thinking, "If only I tried a little harder…"

No matter how hard she tries, the refrain doesn't change.

Can't hold down a job. Can't finish a degree. Can't maintain a relationship. Can't seem to do the things an average adult can do.

"What's wrong with you?"

If only I try a little harder…

Adulthood Will Not be Graded

There is no gifted class in adulthood. No one cares if you can memorize all 20 weekly spelling words after looking at them once. You don't get to escape life on Fridays, reading *MAD* magazine while the sounds of the playground drift in through the open windows.

When you arrive in adulthood lacking the social skills that most people have mastered by sixth grade, life becomes exponentially more confusing and hard to navigate. For much of my adulthood, I've had the odd belief that someday I would "grow up" and suddenly feel like an adult. That I was just a little behind the curve when it came to social skills and one day everything would simply fall into place.

I don't know when or how I was expecting this to happen. It's illogical. Maybe it stems from the belief that social skills are intuitive rather than a skill set that needs to be learned.

Typical people acquire social skills primarily by absorption; autistic people need to be taught social skills explicitly. When we're not, we're no more likely to learn them instinctively than we are to intuitively pick up algebra.

Yes, intelligence helps. In particular, it helps me identify patterns and come up with rules—rules that any neurotypical adult could tell me, if I asked them.

If I thought to ask, which I often don't.

For example, at a get-together at a neighbor's house, I accidentally knocked over a wine glass. The glass broke; I apologized.

Years later, while reading an etiquette book, I learned that I should have offered to replace the glass. This sounds like common sense in retrospect, but it's not a rule I would have intuited or even thought to ask someone about.

Perhaps this is why the invitations for drinks at that neighbor's home abruptly stopped. Did they find me insufferably rude? I have no idea.

Worse, when I mentioned the rule to my daughter, she frowned and said, "You didn't know that?"

There are innumerable unwritten social rules like this one. Generally, I learn a social rule by reading about it, having someone explain it to me or seeing it in action. Unfortunately, many rules are executed privately, so there is no chance for me to observe them. Most adults navigate complex social interactions by employing perspective taking—by putting themselves in the shoes of the other party and intuiting the correct response.

Unfortunately, perspective taking is particularly hard when you're autistic. It has little to do with intelligence and is nearly impossible to fake. Where other adults seem to rely on gut reactions and intuitive responses, I rely on a catalog of past experiences for navigating social interactions. I look for patterns and test out communication strategies like a scientist conducting an experiment. I have 43 years of experimenting behind me and there are days when I still feel like I don't understand even the most basic elements of social communication.

Yes I'm smart, and I'm also developmentally disabled. One does not cancel out the other.

3

Navigating the Social Communication Jungle

Autism is fundamentally a social communication disorder. The more I read about the traits of ASD, the more my lifelong difficulties with social interaction made sense. I'd been called everything from painfully shy and socially awkward to cold and antisocial. Again and again I'd come away from social interactions feeling like I was missing something, some key component of socializing that other people seemed to magically understand.

Now, thanks to my ASD diagnosis, I finally had an explanation for decades of social misfires. In fact, I had many explanations. Determined to sort out the complex web of autistic traits, I threw myself into researching social communication. Some areas of difficulty were familiar: eye contact, body language, small talk, facial expressions. Others sounded foreign and vaguely ominous: face blindness, flat affect, scripting, perspective taking, echolalia.

Slowly, as I made my way through the jungle of social communication deficits, a few key ideas took shape:

- The way I use my face and body to convey information is different from the way typical people communicate nonverbally.

- Even when I pay attention to facial expressions and body language—which I rarely do—they carry little meaning for me.

- My ability to process verbal communication and to communicate with speech is impaired, while my ability to communicate in writing is a strength.

- I've developed unusual ways of navigating social situations, substituting rules, pattern recognition, and scripted language for perspective taking and reading nonverbal communication.

These four realizations helped put a lifetime of social awkwardness into perspective—everything from why I struggle with completing simple everyday transactions with strangers to why I scare small children.

If you think I'm exaggerating, read on.

You Scare Me

A few years ago, my husband and I had some new friends over for lunch. They brought along their two young boys. Toward the end of the meal, the five-year-old, who was sitting next to me, looked at me and said, "You scare me."

This was pre-diagnosis, so like everyone else at the table, I laughed it off as one of those inappropriate things that kids sometimes say.

Still, his comment stayed with me for weeks. I couldn't figure out what I'd done to scare him. He was a friendly, talkative little boy. I'd shown him how to get my dog to do a couple of simple tricks and had given him some bits of hot dog to use as treats. I'd asked him about his swimming lessons and whether he wanted a dog of his own. I'd cooked him a cheeseburger so he wouldn't have to eat the fancy grown-up food. He'd even chosen the seat next to me at lunch. I thought we were getting along great.

And then, out of nowhere, he told me that I was scary. I was more puzzled than offended, but his comment got me thinking about whether there was something strange about how I look to others. Sometimes when I'd catch people staring at me in a restaurant or a store, his words would come back.

"You scare me."

Why?

Months later, I was sorting through boxes of photos and it hit me. There it was—there *I* was—staring back at myself from photo after photo with some variation of a blank, checked-out expression. Standing in front of the Christmas tree. Attending a wedding. On vacation. The people around me are smiling and I have either a blank look or an uncomfortable, when-is-this-going-to-be-over expression. Occasionally, it's obvious I'm faking a smile, which only makes me look like I'm in pain.

I soon discovered that the technical term for my lack of expression is flat or blunted affect, which means that a person displays reduced verbal or nonverbal emotional expressiveness. Some signs of blunted affect are a monotonous tone of voice, a lack of facial expressions or a lack of gestures. Often people with blunted affect respond to emotional situations in unexpected ways or have facial expressions that don't match their feelings. This can cause others to incorrectly assume they are bored, hostile, mad, sad, depressed, or "spaced out" at inappropriate times.

Blunted affect is often unsettling to others and it's frustrating to me. Not only do I have trouble verbalizing my emotions but my face keeps wandering off on its own and freelancing. More than once I've had a professor pause during a lecture to ask me if I had a question. One day, curious why this happened so often, I finally said, "No, why?"

"Because you're frowning," the professor replied.

Surprised at his reply, I blurted out, "I'm not frowning. This is my concentrating face."

The rest of the class laughed, but I was embarrassed. There I was, sitting in calculus class day after day, looking confused, but never asking any questions. This made my professor so uncomfortable that he stopped his lecture to ask me what my problem was. I wonder if he even believed me when I told him I wasn't confused.

HOW CAN YOU TELL IF YOU HAVE FLAT OR BLUNTED AFFECT?

Here are some ways to tell if you have flat or blunted affect:

- Do people ask you why you're sad when you're not sad?*
- Do people ask you why you're angry when you're not angry?*
- Do people say you look bored when you're interested?
- Do people say you look confused when you're concentrating?
- Do people tell you that you're being insensitive or ignoring them when you're actually concerned about them?
- Do people get mad at you because they think you're reacting inappropriately in emotional situations?

These are all signs that how you feel and how you appear to feel aren't matching up, which is a key feature of flat or blunted affect.

*Especially true if what you're feeling at the time is contentment.

When verbal and nonverbal communication don't match, I've found that people are often more inclined to believe the nonverbal cues. Typical people see nonverbal cues as more reliable, believing that even when a person is lying, their body will give them away.

In some situations, a disconnect between verbal and nonverbal communication can be a big liability. What if a job interviewer or a romantic partner interprets it as a sign that you're lying? It can be very difficult to convince them otherwise.

There are two potential solutions to coping with blunted affect. The first is simply to tell people up front. My husband knows that I'm autistic and that my nonverbal communication isn't very reliable. When disclosure isn't an option, many people find that learning to fake facial expressions can be useful. For example, after my professor's comment about my frowning, when I noticed an instructor glancing in my direction too often, I assumed that I was making the confused face and purposely put on my "interested but neutral" face. I also made sure to nod occasionally, which is a positive nonverbal cue.

There are a number of other positive nonverbal cues that you can use as part of an "I'm listening" repertoire to counter blunted affect during one-on-one conversations, including:

- intermittent eye contact
- leaning closer to the speaker
- smiling and nodding
- open arm posture (rather than crossed arms)
- an occasional light touch on the hand, arm, or shoulder.

At first, intentionally employing body language can feel stilted or fake, but with practice it can be a quick, easy way to put strangers at ease. The same is true of making eye contact. If you have difficulty understanding how to convey the right social signals with your eyes, here's a quick primer:

- Sustain eye contact for 4–5 seconds at a time. More than that can indicate that you are trying to intimidate the other person or that you're romantically interested in them.
- Beware of prolonged eye contact. If someone is making prolonged eye contact with you, this may be a signal that the interaction has become more intense than you intended. You can signal disinterest by looking off to the side.
- While you're talking, look to the side or slightly upward when you break eye contact. This indicates thinking. Looking down signals that you're done talking.
- When the other person is talking, break eye contact by shifting your gaze to their mouth rather than looking away. Looking away signals boredom.
- If the other person is talking about something emotional and looks away, you should continue to look at them to show that you care.
- Make eye contact when you are first introduced to someone. Not doing so is interpreted as disrespectful.
- If eye contact feels impossible, try looking at the person's forehead, just above their eyes. This simulates eye contact.

Making eye contact—or, more precisely, not making eye contact—is a big problem for many autistic individuals. The ability to convincingly fake eye contact, while not very helpful for us, puts other people at ease.

Eye Contact: The Conversation Within the Conversation

Why does eye contact seem to matter so much to nonautistic people? Well, for one thing, most humans are hardwired from birth to seek out the eyes of others for important social information. In fact, typical babies naturally seek out the eye regions of people's faces and prefer looking at eyes over other areas of the face or other objects.

WHAT IS THE PURPOSE OF MAKING EYE CONTACT?

Depending on the context, brief intermittent eye contact while interacting with someone:

- acknowledges the other person
- indicates interest
- adds warmth to your words
- provides positive feedback
- encourages them to continue talking
- signals that you are friendly
- suggests you're being polite
- shows respect
- projects confidence
- increases intimacy.

Autistic people of all ages, however, don't seem to have a strong instinct for eye contact. There are many theories to explain our lack of eye contact. However, the one that makes the most sense to me is that we simply don't derive the same type of expressive information from eye contact that nonautistic people do.

For most autistic adults, the "social face" is like a foreign language that we're only somewhat proficient in. I took one semester of Spanish in college. If I watch a Spanish-language program, I can pick out some familiar words and phrases but I don't understand anywhere near as much as a native Spanish speaker.

Facial expressions are the same—I can read the basics. I can decipher the basic emotions like happiness, sadness, surprise, anger, and confusion. More subtle expressions—those that rely heavily on the use of the eyes and the area around the eyes to understand—are much harder.

Because my fluency at reading faces is poor and my facial expression vocabulary is stuck in Faces 101 (i.e. basic), intently studying a conversation partner's face is of little help to me. Like watching Spanish-language TV, there may be a lot of data available, but that doesn't mean I can make sense of it, even when I'm really trying.

Like many people on the spectrum, I've learned to use other information to fill in the blanks when it comes to facial expressions. I often focus on a person's mouth, which I find conveys emotions more explicitly to me than the eyes.

I can gather additional data from tone of voice, especially if I know the person well. Over time, through a variety of interactions, I build up a databank of voice qualities for a person. With enough conversations in the databank, I need only a few words to recognize the happy voice, the fibbing voice, or the "You're not gonna like this" voice.

IS FACE BLINDNESS RELATED TO DIFFICULTY READING FACIAL EXPRESSIONS?

Prosopagnosia, commonly known as face blindness or facial agnosia, is an impairment in the ability to recognize faces. Although there isn't a lot of research to support a conclusive link between ASD and prosopagnosia, some degree of face blindness seems to be common in many autistic adults.

Some of the signs of prosopagnosia are:

- failure to recognize a friend or family member, especially when you encounter them unexpectedly
- tendency to remember or recognize people based on their hairstyle, gait, voice, or other defining non-facial feature
- failure to recognize people out of context
- failure to recognize yourself in the mirror or in photos.

Many autistic adults have alternative ways of recognizing people, including close relatives. For example, I pick my husband out in a crowd by the way he walks or by what I know he's wearing that day. Other useful cues are voice, hairstyle, facial hair, glasses, or body shape.

If we can learn these kinds of work-arounds for reading emotion, why can't we simply learn to read the eyes?

There are programs to teach children on the spectrum how to interpret facial expressions. But for adults, it's a bit more complicated. We've spent decades of our lives not making eye contact. Which raises an interesting question: Are we unable to read the eyes because we don't make eye contact and therefore don't have a rich enough data bank to draw on? Or do we not make eye contact because we discovered early on that the eye region doesn't hold useful data for us and our limited data gathering abilities are better "spent" on areas like (in my case) the mouth or voice?

When you factor in the level of discomfort that many autistic people feel when making eye contact, it's easy to see why learning to use and read the eyes in social interaction can seem like such an overwhelming prospect.

The amount of discomfort that people on the spectrum experience when making eye contact ranges from mild to unbearable. For many autistic adults:

- Eye contact can feel too emotionally intense.
- Eye contact can lead to physical discomfort.
- Making eye contact during a conversation can make it harder to concentrate.

The discomfort often varies from situation to situation. I'm more comfortable making eye contact with people I know very well or hardly at all. People who I know somewhat (professors, fellow students, business acquaintances) are the ones who are the most difficult to look in the eyes.

When I experience discomfort with eye contact, it's more than simply feeling awkward or socially uncomfortable. I literally start to feel that if I look into the person's eyes for even one second longer I'll have to flee the room. The classic "fight or flight" symptoms suggest that my brain is perceiving the sustained eye contact as a threat. Why is this? And why does it happen most strongly with people who I consider acquaintances but not strangers or intimates?

Perhaps it's because I'm self-conscious about the uneven balance of social power. The other person is clearly gathering social data from my eyes but I'm not able to do the same.

Ironically, given my small range of often inappropriate expressions, what they're gathering from me is probably as useless as the fragments of nonverbal communication that I'm picking up from them.

Eye contact with strangers tends to be fleeting and meaningless. The exchange of information feels limited and safe. Eye contact with my husband or daughter, on the other hand, carries none of the social balance of power issues that I feel with acquaintances. I don't need to worry about what they might be discovering about me or whether I'm missing some key nonverbal cue. I know that if I am, they'll tell me.

Acquaintances, however, are still (or sometimes perpetually) in the "getting to know you" stage. We're feeling each other out, gathering data that will determine the course of future interactions and cement our perceptions of each other.

For nonautistic people, eye contact is a rich and layered language. It's the conversation within the conversation. Autistic individuals are largely deaf to this language. It's no wonder it makes us so uncomfortable when others try to speak to us with their eyes.

Social Use of Language

Nonverbal communication is often cited as being a significant part of social interaction. Various studies have tried to measure exactly how much information we glean from nonverbal cues and come up with figures ranging from 50 to 80 percent. For those of us who project atypical, nonverbal cues and have a limited ability to process what other people are saying with their eyes and body, those are scary statistics.

There's a good chance we're missing more than half of what people are communicating to us and that's before taking into consideration our difficulties with pragmatics, the social use of language. Although many autistic people, particularly those diagnosed with Asperger's, begin speaking at a typical age (or even early) pragmatic impairments are nearly universal in ASD.

WHAT ARE PRAGMATICS?

Pragmatics or pragmatic language refers to the way we use language for social interaction. Pragmatic skills include:

- introducing, maintaining and changing topics of conversation
- greeting others
- entering and exiting conversations
- asking questions
- taking turns in conversation
- asking for and supplying clarifying information
- using language appropriate to the age of the listener
- modulating volume and word choice based on the situation
- asking for and offering help at appropriate times
- avoiding repetitious or irrelevant information
- using humor.

Although I was well aware of my awkwardness in conversation—especially when it came to small talk, especially with strangers—I was surprised to learn I have a serious pragmatic impairment. Surprised, not because I believed I was good at conversation, but because I thought I was good with words.

What I didn't realize is that I'm good with *written* words. When I write, I can take as much time as I need to shape my thoughts into a coherent whole. I can get feedback from others to check for clarity. I can let an idea breathe and grow over days or weeks.

Doing this in a spoken conversation is impossible. There's no delete button for spoken words. Revising, in the form of explanations and clarifications, is often unsuccessful. Once you say something, it's out there in a way that is, ironically, indelible.

In the past year, I've learned that my verbal processing—both receptive and expressive—is impaired. The evidence? I often need more time than the average person to understand or respond to spoken words. I struggle with verbal instructions. If there's background noise or other distractions, my auditory processing lags to the point that it can take a few seconds to process speech from noise into words. My verbal responses default to scripts or become minimal when the conversation takes an unexpected turn, moves too fast or is too unstructured.

THE TELEPHONE: A SPECIAL KIND OF COMMUNICATION PROBLEM

When I first saw the question, "Do you dislike talking on the phone?" on an Asperger's Syndrome screening questionnaire, I was mystified (and more than a little relieved). Does Asperger's Syndrome cause people to dislike the phone? What a strange and specific condition, I thought to myself.

When someone says, "I'll call you," my first reaction is, "What can I do to make that not happen?" This is especially true of social calls, the kind that many women think are a pleasant way to connect with a friend. Business calls are less stressful because they have a goal and I can formulate a script ahead of time. Assuming the call goes mostly to script and is short, I can power through it.

The phone should be an ideal means of communication for someone who isn't good at reading body language or making eye contact. All you get over the phone is a voice, right? Communication distilled to its essence: words.

But why should something as simple as phone call require "powering through" like the social equivalent of an Ironman triathlon?

Unlike written communication, which is truly just words, phone conversation relies heavily on prosody (the rhythm, stress, or intonation of speech). Prosody often conveys the emotional content of language or signals the presence of irony, sarcasm, emphasis, or contrast.

Suddenly, this one aspect of speech looks pretty important, doesn't it?

If you can't interpret prosody, you don't get certain types of humor, you miss the subtle emotional shifts in the conversation, you fail to recognize which details are being emphasized. That's just on the listening end. If your own speaking voice lacks prosody—a common autistic trait—your conversation partner will probably feel ill at ease too. Throw in pragmatic impairments like difficulty with turn taking and changing topics and you get phone conversations punctuated by, "No, you go ahead" and...

"What were you going to say?" and the much loved, "Are you still there?"

I've also noticed that I have a tendency to pause for too long before my turn to speak, which makes the other person anxious. He or she will start speaking again, often right as I start to reply to the previous comment or question. This results in a lot of false starts, interruptions and awkward "No, *you* go first" encouragement.

Sometimes I miss the verbal cue, like a change in intonation, that indicates the other person has finished and it's my turn to talk. Sometimes I'm using that long pause to collect my thoughts or compose a reply. If the conversation is particularly unstructured, I may start to drift off and lose track of it altogether.

If I know that these ill-timed pauses are the problem, why don't I do something about it? Good question. Since discovering why I struggle with social conversations, I've begun to work on improving my turn-taking skills on the phone. Progress has been slow, though. Like reading facial expressions or making eye contact, the nuances of pragmatic language can be hard to learn as an adult.

Spoken communication is much less forgiving than written communication, particularly spoken communication with people I've just met. There is a moment I dread in conversations with strangers.

It doesn't happen with every stranger, but it happens often enough that I can pinpoint the moment a conversation turns. To start, we're both on our best interacting-with-a-stranger behavior, a bit wary, a bit too friendly, overly polite. Then I make a grave pragmatic slip. I miss key information, ask the other person to repeat something one too many times, stutter, backtrack, repeat myself, interrupt *again*, lose the thread of the conversation.

The response—the one that makes my skin heat up and my heart race and the blood in my ears pound—is subtle but sudden. The other person begins speaking more slowly, repeating important points, using smaller words or asking questions like, "Are you following me?" and "Does that make sense?"

In other words, they make a pragmatic shift, adjusting their language to accommodate my pragmatic impairment. While their adjustment is warranted, it's also frustrating because there is a significant disconnect between the way I present verbally and my intelligence.

In short, I look better on paper. If I was a shelter pup, there would be a note in my file that said, "Does not show well."

Generally, this isn't a problem. I've engineered my work life so that I first encounter people via email or some other text-based correspondence. By the time we talk on the phone or face to face, the other person has (I hope) formed an opinion of me that will withstand my verbal glitches.

I've gravitated toward text-based media in general, spending my days working primarily with the written word. Still, I have to do things like go to the doctor, contact the super in my building for repairs, and navigate the university records office to correct my transcript—all situations where I've encountered the dreaded pragmatic shift.

Each time it happens, I want to tell the other person that my poor verbal communication has no impact on my ability to understand the way a ground fault interrupter works or what the risk factors for breast cancer are or how to read my college transcript. I don't need to have these things explained to me like I'm a child.

Because that's often what happens. People make an ill-considered leap from "poor language skills" to "not very smart." In an ideal world, people would adjust their communication in ways that are helpful to those of us with pragmatic impairments without being condescending. How?

Here is my wish list:

- Be patient. I might need a little extra time to compose my answer or to process what's been said.
- If I ask for clarification, try explaining in a different way. If I didn't understand the way something was explained the first time, an exact repetition probably won't help.
- Assume that if I don't understand something, I'll say so.
- Don't rely on my body language or other typical cues for feedback about whether I understand. Unless you're also autistic or know me very well, you probably can't read my body language any better than I can read yours.
- Give me time to write down key information.
- Don't oversimplify your language or speak unusually slowly or loudly.
- When giving me verbal instructions, break them down into specific steps and explain one step at a time.
- If I keep repeating a question or statement, I need a stronger acknowledgment that you've heard and understood me.
- Treat me like a competent adult.

Except for this last one—which is a courtesy that all adults should afford other adults—these are accommodations. Because they are outside the norm and others may not know that I find them helpful, I need to ask rather than simply expecting others to guess what I need.

This is an area that I still find difficult to navigate. In fact, asking for help and asking for clarification are pragmatic skills. Asking for help with pragmatics is bit like trying to drive your car to the gas station for a fill-up when the tank is completely empty.

4

A Complicated Relationship with Relationships

Like many autistic people, I have a complicated relationship with relationships. I've been married for more years than I've been single. I've had close friends on and off throughout my life. I have an adult daughter who I enjoy spending time with.

Yet I can be alone in a crowded room as easily as in an empty room. Even as a kid, when I had to be with people, I managed to somehow be alone. When my family visited my aunt and uncle's house, I liked to spend the visit playing solitaire at the table with the grown-ups while the other kids played outside.

My aunt, a fellow solitaire player, taught me complicated variations of the game. She taught me how to build card houses. She gave me Barbie coloring books and showed me how to use a ruler to make plaid dresses for the Barbies using colorful patterns of straight lines. Some nights I spent the visit making every single item of clothing in a coloring book plaid.

When I grew too old for coloring, I retreated to my older cousin's room. She loaned me books to read and albums to listen to, fueled my obsession with *The Doors* and my love for rock and roll. When she went out with her friends for the evening, she closed the door and left me lying on her bed with the music turned up and my head buried in a book. When it was time to go, my parents would send my sister up to retrieve me.

While my parents encouraged me to have more friends, they didn't seem especially concerned about my tendency to do things alone. It was the 1970s. Parents weren't expected to know what their kids were doing 24/7. There was an element of benign neglect to 1970s parenting that was a blessing in disguise for a young Aspie.

Eventually, as I got older and started spending every moment at home in my room with the door closed, my parents began to grow concerned. They instituted rules about when I could close my door and how much time I could spend in my room. By this point, adolescence was in full swing and I'd started having meltdowns. I think my parents assumed my isolation was responsible for my emotional instability, but in fact the opposite was true. The more they tried to get me to interact, the more emotionally fragile I became.

I started lying about where I was going, saying I was riding my bike to a friend's house when I was just going out to ride around alone. At a time when my friends were hiding sex and drinking and drugs from their parents, I was hiding my need to be alone.

Already I understood that "alone" was a word that carried a stigma. Alone is for people who can't figure out how to make friends or maintain relationships. That certainly applied to me in some ways. When I look back on the kids I was friends with, we were all odd in some way. Not many kids wanted to be friends with the girl who had three fingers on each hand or the girl with albinism or the girl who had seizures or the boy who ate paste and blew his nose in the hair of a pencil troll named Ned.

Or the geeky girl with the undiagnosed Asperger's.

I had no idea there was anything unusual about any of these kids. I also didn't realize that I wasn't supposed to be friends with them. According to unspoken social rules, I later learned, making friends with the weird kids means you're weird too. This was completely lost on me. I liked them and I was grateful that they liked me back.

Some people might have looked at us and thought, "How nice that those kids have each other so they aren't lonely," but I would have been just as content to be alone. I learned early on that there were ways of being alone that snuck under the adults' radar. For example, it was easy to get out of recess—just volunteer to help out in the library or the reading teacher's office at lunchtime. I got to be alone and I scored brownie points with the grown-ups.

As I got older, this became harder to pull off. Sucking up to teachers is okay in third grade. By middle school, it makes you a target of ridicule. That's when being alone gets harder. That's when the stigma of alone started to become undeniably obvious.

If you look up "alone" in a thesaurus, you'll find a long list of negative and depressing synonyms: abandoned, companionless, deserted, desolate, detached, forlorn, forsaken, friendless, hermit, isolated, lonely, lonesome…

Ironically, the times in my life that I've experienced this type of aloneness—the lonely, companionless isolation—I've nearly always been surrounded by people. I still remember how I felt stepping off the bus at the YMCA camp on the day of my fifth grade year-end field trip. The other kids scattered immediately and I was left with the sinking realization that they'd planned their activities—and secured partners for them—in advance. I wandered a bit until I found a deserted swing set—fifth graders don't play on the swings—and was soon joined by the kid who would try to hang himself at recess the following year.

Later, I joined the nature hike, played tennis with some kids from another school who needed a fourth player, went swimming by myself, and was told that I sucked at ping-pong and should go do something else. I spent most of that day feeling lonely, though I was surrounded by my fifth grade class.

Yet, when I'm alone, I rarely feel lonely. If I were writing the thesaurus entries for alone, the synonyms would include: authentic, free, individual, indulgent, open, peaceful, protected, pure, quiet, rejuvenating, solitary.

Thanks to the amount of time I spend alone, I'm on intimate terms with myself. I have a running internal dialogue that informs my life, my writing, my relationships. I observe and absorb the world around me. I'm good at being alone. The sense of inner security this creates is one of the hidden gifts of Asperger's.

A Cycle of Shrinking and Growing

When I've made friends as an adult, it's always been via a common interest. In fact, that's how I met my husband Sang.

When I was in my 20s, newly married with a young child, I tried befriending the moms of my daughter's friends. That was what the women I was surrounded by seemed to be doing. In fact, they made it look easy. Chatting in the hallway of the church basement while waiting to pick up their toddlers from playgroup. Bonding over potty training and nap schedules. Making play dates and planning outings to the park.

I quickly realized that making friends that way wasn't for me. I have no idea how adults maintain a "random" friendship, which is how I think of friendships that don't revolve around a shared interest. A common interest not only gives me a starting point for conversations, it creates a ready-made activity for spending time together. It's much easier for me to manage conversation during the breaks in a dog training class than while sitting down with someone over coffee.

The problem with making friends through common interests, though, is that if my current interests are solitary pursuits, I'm unlikely to have any current friends. When I was involved in martial arts class, I had friends in the class. Now I run and swim for exercise, activities that I prefer not to do with a group. That means I don't have anyone in my life who fits the conventional definition of a friend. I don't see this as a problem and Sang never has either.

So I was startled when, about six months after my diagnosis, Sang said, "I'm concerned that your world is shrinking."

Shrinking implies something was once larger or more abundant. In the two decades we've been married, we've often struggled to compromise between his desire for social interaction and my natural aversion to social occasions. But he'd never expressed concern over how little I need to be around people.

It was true that I was spending an unusual amount of time at home, alone. Two years earlier, I'd been finishing up my long-put-off university degree. That meant spending three days a week on campus, surrounded by people. Sang and I also had frequent social engagements because we lived in an area where we knew quite a few people. Well, mostly he knew people and I got invited because adult social engagements tend to be couples events.

Compared to the years I was attending school, my days post-diagnosis were simpler and less social. Most days I would wake up, work out, write, work, eat a few times in between. Because I work at home, some days the car never left the garage. The geography of my social interaction was much smaller than it had been when I was going to school or in the years before that, when my daughter was younger, or when I was working at a job that required interacting face to face with people all day.

Looking back over my life, there is a consistent pattern of my social sphere shrinking and growing. In the years leading up to my realization that I might be autistic, I went through a period when my world shrunk to a very small place. Sang and I moved far away from our roots, to the desert, to a place so remote that we regularly encountered coyotes on our evening walks and the nearest gas station—the nearest anything—was a 15-minute drive.

In that place, I found a deep internal sense of quiet. I let go of a lot of old hurts. I started to understand myself.

Of course, life gradually crept in again. We formed ties. We put down new roots. I decided to go back to school. Gradually I began to feel a creeping sense of unease. The quiet I'd found receded as I was forced out of that peaceful place I'd created for myself. One by one, I backed out of the rooms in my mind, turned off the lights and closed the doors, shutting away the parts of myself that I instinctively sensed wouldn't survive being exposed to the outside world.

Until something inside me rebelled and refused to close another door. In retrospect, that internal rebellion—the tension that arose between the security of the peaceful place I'd found and the stimulation of the outside world I was being drawn back into—was the first step toward discovering that I'm autistic.

I didn't know that then. All I knew was that something had to give.

The tension grew in a way it hadn't before. I became acutely aware of the two very different head spaces I lived in. There was this new space, which existed mostly when I was alone, that felt very natural. It was secure and comfortable and, most of all, quiet. I hadn't been in a place that internally quiet in a very long time, certainly not since I'd reached an age that had two digits in it.

Then there was the other head space, the one I'd taken for granted as being life, the one where I had a stranglehold on everything to keep it from flying apart. It pushed me to grow and expand myself, but at the same time I lacked the natural ease I felt when I was alone.

Looking back, I can see that ASD has been the root cause of my lifelong social dissonance. I've always known that I'm different, but not precisely how or why. This caused me to feel like I was simply a failure at relationships. Even the one relationship that I would consider the most successful in my life—my marriage—has been a long, hard road filled with moments where I questioned my ability to relate to another person in any sort of "normal" way.

Marriage: The Longest, Hardest, and Best Relationship of All

Being married to someone on the spectrum is challenging. Some people might go so far as to say it's impossible. A quick internet search on 'Asperger's marriage' will turn up plenty of horror stories. As my husband would tell you, being married to someone with undiagnosed ASD is even more difficult. Without the explanation of Asperger's and an understanding of the social communication impairments that accompany it, it's natural for the nonautistic partner to assume that the autistic partner is being intentionally rude, selfish, cold, controlling, and a host of other negative things.

Before my diagnosis, there was a frequent pattern in my marriage: I would unknowingly do something hurtful, then be surprised when Sang was upset by it. This inevitably triggered a downward spiral, Sang assuming I was being intentionally hurtful—because how could a grown adult not realize that it was hurtful—and me feeling bewildered about what exactly I'd done to cause so much upset.

Often these discussions stalemated in a conversational dead end. I would sink into a shutdown or meltdown, where my only verbal response was, "I don't know," and Sang would resort to a frustrated refrain of "I don't understand you." Even typing those two phrases is hard because they bring back memories of some of the most difficult times in our marriage.

All of the things that make life with ASD challenging also complicate life with an autistic partner: communication challenges, sensory sensitivities, attachment to routines. If one partner is neurotypical (NT) and the other is autistic, it may soon become obvious that they have very different expectations regarding socializing, intimacy, and having children. An ASD–NT marriage is essentially a cross-cultural partnership, and like any cross-cultural exchange, it can be a rewarding experience or a nightmare.

Many couples, however, make it work. Some are naturally suited to accepting or working around each other's needs. Some attend couples counseling, turning to a dispassionate third party for help in navigating thorny issues. Being stubborn and independent sorts, Sang and I have often learned the hard way what works for us.

In retrospect, my Asperger's diagnosis is one of the best things that ever happened in our marriage. So much of what we'd struggled with suddenly made sense. In the past year, we've learned that there are many things we can each work on improving and some things that we'll just have to accept. Best of all, Sang no longer says, "I don't understand you" and I hardly ever say, "I don't know."

Instead we have conversations that start out like this recent one:

Sang: I know you didn't mean to, but when you said that, it made me angry and I'd like to understand what you were thinking.

Me: I'm sorry that made you angry. You're right, I didn't mean it that way. Here's what was going through my head...

This is so much healthier than the painful misunderstandings we used to have. We still argue and hurt each other the way couples do, but now we have a framework for understanding why we approach our relationship so differently. We've learned a lot about making an ASD–NT marriage work over the years. I hope some of the lessons we've learned—often the hard way—will be helpful for other couples where one partner is on the spectrum.

12 Lessons from an ASD–NT Marriage

1. *Dividing up household and family responsibilities according to each partner's strengths is empowering.* Everyone has strengths and weaknesses. For example, I'm good at organizing and scheduling. I suck at ironing. I have the patience to help with homework and sit through two-hour soccer practices. I should never be allowed to handle power tools. I enjoy the research involved in managing the household finances. The thought of calling up a neighbor to confirm that we'll be attending a party causes me to procrastinate for days and need a nap afterward.

   Fortunately, I have a partner who has very different strengths and weaknesses. Dividing up the household responsibilities accordingly has made both of our lives easier and addressed one of the biggest potential pitfalls in an ASD–NT relationship: the potential for the NT partner to feel like a caregiver rather than a spouse and lover. Because I have clearly designated responsibilities that I excel at, delegating my weak areas to my partner feels less like a failing and more like an equal partnership. Successful partnerships are built on a rational division of labor and a marriage is no different.

2. *Sometimes you have to apologize, even if you're not sure why.* There are times when it's hard to see why something is hurtful. I've learned that it doesn't matter if what I said or did was unintentional. It doesn't matter if I meant well. It doesn't matter if I think it's silly or meaningless. I just apologize.

   This can be difficult. My first instinct is often to say, "But that's not what I meant" or "What's the big deal?" This is a bad idea. If my words or actions hurt my partner, then it is a big deal. Ideally, when this happens, Sang will be able to calmly identify what I did and how that made him feel: "I feel hurt when you point out in front of other people that I wasn't paying attention to the conversation." That gives me the opportunity to calmly consider his point of view and apologize: "I'm sorry. I didn't realize that would bother you. I'll try not to do it in the future."

   Obviously, having this conversation calmly and lovingly can be a hard place to get to. For a long time, Sang thought I had a mean streak. After learning more about Asperger's, he began to understand that my brain's atypical wiring is responsible for a lot of the hurtful things I say. Now he tries to calmly point out when he feels that I'm being insensitive.

   We've both accepted that even when he tells me that something bothers him, I may still do it again. I'll try not to, but there's no guarantee because ASD makes it hard for me to generalize from one situation to the next. There's a good chance I'll say something similar without realizing it's hurtful, because in my mind it's not the exact same thing. It takes a leap of faith for the NT partner to give the autistic partner the benefit of the doubt when this happens, but this kind of trust may be one of the things that saves a marriage in the end.

3. *Autistic people have good days and bad days.* Anxiety or sensory overload can aggravate a wide variety of ASD traits. When I'm stressed I find that I'm more clumsy, less open to being touched, more rigid in my thinking, less willing to deviate from routine, more vulnerable to perseverative thinking, more prone to tunnel vision, and more likely to struggle with auditory processing.

   Traits that don't normally interfere with my functioning can become a big obstacle. This can be hard for a neurotypical partner to understand or accept. I'm sure that the last thing my husband wants to deal with in the middle of a crisis is an outbreak of my autistic traits. But we both have accepted that I don't have a lot of control over when or how my functional capacity degrades under stress. He does his best to support me and I do my best to manage myself until the crisis passes.

4. *Sensory sensitivities might mean you have to get creative in the bedroom.* Touching, one of the most important and fundamental aspects of an intimate relationship, can be uncomfortable for autistic people. Certain types of touching—especially light or unexpected touches—are more likely to be uncomfortable. Discovering what types of touch each partner likes and doesn't like is essential to having a healthy sex life. (More on this under "Sensory Sensitivities" in Chapter 7.)

5. *Spontaneous affection can be challenging when you're on the spectrum.* Spontaneous affection is often included in lists of "ways to keep a marriage alive." It's also often included in lists of ways to trigger withdrawal in an Aspie. So what's a married Aspie to do?

   I've found that it's hard to change how I feel about being touched at the "wrong" time. When I'm stressed, anxious or intensely engaged in an activity, being touched often registers as an unwanted distraction rather than spontaneous affection. There's a good chance I'll push Sang away or respond stiffly if he approaches me at a time when my brain is in hands-off mode.

   There are also times when my brain is so busy trying to figure out where a certain type of touch is headed that it's hard to simply relax and enjoy the moment. Because I don't always get the nonverbal cues involved in intimacy, I sometimes rely on the intellectual side of my brain to process how an intimate moment is going to proceed. Yeah, that's as romantic as it sounds.

   While it's hard to alter my instinctive responses to spontaneous affection, I try to compensate by initiating physical contact that I'm comfortable with at a time that's good for me.

   Author Liane Holliday Willey once took a lot of heat for including holding her husband's hand five times a day on her "to-do" list. Putting handholding on a to-do list may sound cold and mechanical but that doesn't mean that the action itself has to be mechanical. Since I've begun consciously looking for opportunities to initiate small touches during the day, I find that being physically affectionate has become more of a natural instinct for me and that feels good.

6. *Sometimes the NT partner will need to compensate for the autistic partner's social skills deficits.* No matter how hard I work at improving my social skills, I regularly miss nonverbal cues, resulting in everything from confused looks and awkward pauses to downright hostility from other people. This often leaves my husband with the task of "cleaning up after me" socially.

   I also rely on him to take care of certain household responsibilities that require social interaction—especially when it comes to negotiating a purchase or registering a complaint, two areas that are my weakest.

   We all have skills that come naturally and social skills aren't on the list of natural talents for Aspies. We can study and practice and improve, but it's unlikely we'll reach the sort of social proficiency that most neurotypical adults have. As an adult it can be hard to rely on a partner to repair social errors. We've found that acceptance can go a long way in situations where change is slow and inconsistent.

7. *Aspies need plenty of alone time.* Being alone is how autistic people regroup. When I retreat to my home office and close the door, it doesn't mean I don't enjoy the company of my family. It has nothing to do with how much I love my husband. It doesn't mean that I'm disinterested, selfish, cold, or insensitive. It means I've hit my limit for social interaction and need to recharge.

   Somehow, Sang figured this out years before we knew anything about Asperger's. He has learned how to recognize when I'm nearing my limit, sometimes before I do. If we have guests staying with us for a few days, he makes a point to build time alone for me into the schedule. If he sees that I'm starting to tire or withdraw during a long social event, he'll suggest that we do something away from the crowd for a short time to help me refocus. He's also come to accept that when I say I need to leave a social situation, I've truly stuck it out as long as I can, and staying longer is going to cost me more than it's worth.

It would be easy for him to see me as a social tyrant. I'm certainly not the sort of wife who thrives on entertaining and socializing. But I've learned that being realistic about my limits—and pushing at them where I can—is less destructive to our relationship than overreaching and ending up in tears.

8. *Compromise is good.* Compromising in a relationship can be hard. I've found taking a cost-benefit approach helpful. What is doing this for my partner going to cost me? What would my not doing it cost him? What are the potential benefits—for him, for me, for our relationship? By listing the costs and benefits as concretely as possible, it's easier for me to find places where I can compromise.

   For example, Sang and I have concluded—after much arguing, discussing, and agonizing—that it's unrealistic to expect that I'll attend every social event we get invited to (his preference). It's also unrealistic for me to attend none of them (my preference). Our compromise is that I'll attend the important events and he'll go to the less important events alone. This means that I'm going to be uncomfortable some of the time (talking to strangers—oh no!) and he's going to be uncomfortable at times (making excuses for my absence). Like most compromises, neither of us is completely happy with this arrangement, but it's the least bad option.

9. *Triggers are real and they aren't going away.* Autistic people often have triggers—experiences that elicit a stress response. Some people have many and others just a

few. Triggers can be environmental/sensory (sounds, smells), social (crowds, public speaking), or situational (new places, unexpected changes). Some triggers are mild. They cause discomfort or low-level anxiety, but we can live with them for a short time if we have to. Others are more severe, leading to meltdowns or withdrawal.

Triggers may seem odd or even incomprehensible to the NT partner. However, Sang and I have learned that no matter how odd a trigger seems, it's important that I communicate my triggers to him and that we find ways to respect my needs and accommodate them when necessary.

Sometimes an accommodation is as simple as the neurotypical partner not explaining *again* why something would be fine if only the Aspie would give it a try. Other accommodations can be more stressful on a relationship. If an Aspie partner can only get a good night's sleep by sleeping alone or she finds grocery stores intolerable, both partners need to be open and honest about what kind of accommodations are feasible.

10. *Communication will be hard. Don't give up.* ASD is a minefield of communication challenges. For years, Sang was certain he was communicating clearly with me but most of what he was saying wasn't truly getting through. Often, neurotypical people communicate in subtle ways that autistic people find difficult to interpret. In particular, body language, facial expressions, and implied communication can be hard for people on the spectrum to interpret correctly.

    For example, I had no idea until recently that when someone walks into the kitchen and says, "Oh, those cookies smell delicious" they're hinting that they would like me to offer them a cookie. My usual response of "thank you" followed by continuing to clean up the kitchen or change the subject is seen by most neurotypical people as cold and rude.

Aspies need explicit communication. Forget about dropping hints. Forget about body language and inferences. We need to be told exactly what our NT partner wants, needs, or expects. And we may need to be told more than once, in slightly different ways.

11. *There are many ways to express love.* Aspies and NTs speak different languages when it comes to expressions of love. Aspies are more likely to express love through practical actions, whereas neurotypical people are more likely to express love through words or symbolic actions. This can be confusing for both partners in an ASD–NT relationship. If you don't learn to translate your partner's "love language" you might spend the rest of your marriage wondering if the person you're sleeping next to every night really, actually loves you.

    How does this translation work? Like this:

    Sang: You don't have to make my lunch every morning. I can pick something up in the cafeteria.

    Me: I don't mind. It only takes a few minutes and I know you'd rather have something healthy to eat. This way you don't have to waste time waiting in line.

    Sang: So you mean you make my lunch because you care about me?

    Me: Exactly.

12. *There are things I'll never understand about my partner.* No matter how long we live together or how much we love each other, I know there will be moments when we both

> feel like we're married to the most incomprehensible person on Earth. Autistic and neurotypical brains have key differences. Understanding this has at least reduced the amount of frustration I feel when Sang does something that leaves me scratching my head.
>
> For example, when he told me that he feels something—a physical sensation of warmth was how he described it—when he says, "I love you" I was stunned. I tell him that I love him every day but I've never associated a physical feeling with those words. I can logically understand what this physical feeling might be like, but I'll probably never know exactly what he feels.
>
> By the same token, I can tell him that when I sit in a crowded restaurant, my brain is tracking the conversations at all of the tables within earshot, but I don't think he can ever replicate that experience in his own head. We can make educated guesses at what's going on with our partner, but there will always be some experiences that we can't truly understand.

When faced with the day-to-day challenges of an ASD–NT marriage, it would be easy for both partners to simply give up in frustration. I can think of plenty of times when walking away would have been easier and less painful than trying to work things out.

Balancing realistic expectations—by both partners—with a concerted effort to improve can be a relationship-saver. Realistic expectations go both ways. The neurotyipcal partner shouldn't expect the autistic partner to morph into a typical person overnight. (Sang says he wouldn't want this even it were possible. Awwwww.)

By the same token, the autistic partner shouldn't expect the NT partner to simply put up with an endless barrage of unchecked autistic traits. Knowing what can be changed and what can be tolerated or accepted is essential.

The day I explained to Sang about Asperger's, one of the first things he said was, "I love you exactly the way you are." I treasure that and I know it's not something he said just to make me feel better. He means it.

I also know that I'm hard to live with. I find *myself* hard to live with at times. Over the past year, I've made a lot of changes in my life. Ideally, I'd like to struggle less on a daily basis and I want the people around me—the people I love—to struggle less too. When it comes to relationships, I've learned that this often requires a delicate balance of adaptation and acceptance.

5

Parenting Aspie Style

In the early days of suspecting that I might have Asperger's, I first shared my suspicion with Sang. After talking it over, he agreed that he saw a lot of Asperger's traits in me. That gave me the confidence to tell my daughter, Jess, who was in her early 20s at the time.

She laughed it off at first, like maybe I just needed to be talked out of this crazy idea that there was something wrong with me. I'd always been different from other moms. We both knew that. But the idea that I might be autistic was, understandably, a lot to process.

Gradually, as I explained more about Asperger's and described common traits, she started coming up with specific examples of times when I'd done something particularly autistic. Some were funny, others less so.

The more we talked about it, the more relieved she sounded. Asperger's syndrome can explain a lot of puzzling behavior, for both the Aspie and the people closest to him or her.

At one point in the conversation, Jess said, "But you're so smart!"

Armed with the reading I'd done, I explained the gap between intellectual intelligence and social aptitude that I'd struggled with all my life. I find it a lot easier to learn calculus than to make small talk. There isn't a lot of carry over between one type of skill and the other.

Jess was quiet for a moment. I'm sure that among other things she was puzzled over why I was so excited to be telling her that I have a developmental disorder. It doesn't sound like a cause for celebration, but I was still in the early flush of discovery. Suddenly so much of my life made sense. I felt like someone had finally given me the user's manual to my brain.

I hadn't yet realized how little I knew about Asperger's or myself. I hadn't yet realized that the user's manual was missing a few key pages. Pages that I'd eventually have to write myself.

The next question Jess asked made that clear. "So, wait, does that mean you don't have feelings?"

When a stranger or acquaintance asks this, it's easy to attribute it to ignorance. One of the most common misconceptions about autistic people is that they're cold and emotionless. But when your own child asks you if you have feelings, well, that's one of those times when the reality of ASD hits and hits hard.

That's when 24 years of not saying, "I love you"—24 years of struggling to express my feelings to my own child—crystallized into one perfect moment of regret, of wishing I'd known all along that there was a reason for how difficult I find it to express what I'm feeling. Because the feelings are there. They may not be quite what the typical mom feels, but I'm absolutely certain that I love my daughter. And I want her to be absolutely certain too.

Unconventional Parenting

I know I haven't been a perfect mother but I also know that the perfect mother doesn't exist. As parents, we all—autistic and nonautistic alike—do the best we can under often challenging circumstances. I have, however, learned that autistic parents face some specific challenges that most parents don't.

Having an autistic parent in the family can be a mixed bag. As parents, we tend to be unconventional. This can mean anything from having an unusual way of expressing love to being the kind of parent who will spend weeks helping their child build a scale model replica of the Island of Sodor out of Lego®.

The effect of an autistic parent on a family may be positive or negative, but most likely it will be some of each. While I wasn't aware that I was autistic when my daughter was growing up, I faced the same challenges that other autistic parents face, including:

- *Sensory sensitivities*: Adults on the spectrum can be sensitive to certain types of light, noise, or smells. With children in the house, limiting things like the sound of the television, the level of noise during a play date or the smells that a baby produces can be difficult. It may be necessary for the autistic parent to have a quiet place they can escape to when necessary to regroup or for the family to divide up household responsibilities to accommodate the autistic parent's sensitivities.

- *Social communication deficits*: Social communication is a big part of parenting. At home, parents are constantly communicating with their children, whether it's to discipline them, to let them know that they're loved or to explain a difficult homework assignment. Away from home, children rely on their parents to advocate for them at school and show them how to get along in the world. When a parent struggles with social communication, it may be necessary for them to seek assistance, either from their partner or another trusted family member.

- *Household management*: Executive function difficulties can make it hard to stay personally organized, let alone keep a household of three or more people running smoothly. Many families with a parent on the spectrum rely heavily on organizational aids like family calendars, reminder lists, and routines to stay on track.

- *Love and support*: Aspies often have an unusual way of showing love and bonding with others. For example, many people on the spectrum are naturally drawn to practical gestures of love and support, such as solving a problem or doing something helpful for a loved one. If a child finds it difficult to understand an Aspie parent's bonding style (or any aspect of their parenting), it may help for both parents to explain that Mom / Dad's brain is wired differently and that's why they do X instead of Y.

Beyond the general challenges that autistic parents of both genders encounter, autistic mothers face some special hurdles. These potential challenges may begin to emerge during pregnancy and quickly intensify with the arrival of the baby. Because I had no idea that I was autistic, I found that motherhood had a particularly steep learning curve.

Infancy and Motherhood

For autistic parents, a new baby is basically all of the things we struggle to cope with wrapped up in one adorable package.

Caring for a baby challenges your sensory sensitivities, messes with your routines, and takes up every spare minute of the day. Babies, and later toddlers, are unpredictable, messy, and demanding. Sometimes they're smelly or noisy. And they don't seem to come with an off switch.

They don't care if mom is sleep-deprived or suffering from sensory overload, if she finds breastfeeding painful or needs a couple of hours of alone time to regroup. When you throw in postpartum hormonal fluctuations and the challenges of

ASD, it's no surprise that the result can be epic meltdowns more fit for a toddler than a new mother.

When Jess was a baby, there were days when I felt like I was going to lose my mind if she didn't stop crying. I remember one day in particular when I found myself standing in the dining room, sobbing uncontrollably and repeatedly banging my head against the wall. If you've ever seen an autistic child have a meltdown, it probably looked much the same. I can only imagine how terrifying this must have been for my husband—watching the mother of his child regress to that point. Particularly since neither of us knew that I was autistic at the time.

But instead of losing his temper or fleeing, he was there to rescue me before I could slip too far into that abyss. When my natural instinct was to withdraw, he kept me tethered to reality in a concrete way that allowed me to stay connected to Jess.

One of the keys to surviving the first months of motherhood as an autistic mom is having that kind of support—both practical help and emotional support—when you reach a crisis point. All new moms need time to themselves to regroup, but for autistic moms this is especially important.

Honestly, there were times when I felt like I couldn't cope with the demands of being a parent for even one more second. Faced with a baby who wouldn't stop crying or wouldn't settle down for a much anticipated nap or was in the mood to play when I was exhausted, I was quick to beat myself up for being a bad mom.

Now I know that my guilt and shame were misplaced. Needing a time out didn't make me a bad parent. It's okay—healthy, in fact—for an autistic parent to ask for help from a partner, relative or babysitter. If I'd known that I was autistic, I would have been more conscientious about asking for this kind of respite. I function much better when I'm not overloaded and that makes me a better parent.

RESCUE STRATEGIES FOR NEW PARENTS

What about those times when a new parent is home alone with their child and can't call on one of the supportive people in their life for help? It's a good idea to have some strategies on hand for de-escalating stress. Fortunately, many of things that babies and toddlers find calming may also be soothing for people on the spectrum.

Here are a few options that I found helpful as a new Aspie mom:

- *A rocking chair*: Many autistic adults find rocking to be soothing and when you're doing it with a baby in a rocking chair, no one looks at you funny. A comfy rocker was one the first things I put on my wish list as a mom-to-be. It became my go-to soothing option for me and Jess in those early months.
- *Music*: Singing to your baby, dancing around the living room with your toddler, or enjoying a favorite song together can all be soothing. For a few months, the only thing that put my infant daughter to sleep at night was U2's *Joshua Tree* album. It wasn't exactly Baby Mozart but we both found it relaxing.
- *Water*: Many autistic people find water calming. If you have access to a swimming pool, you and your child might enjoy spending time in the water together. Once your toddler is old enough, you may find that she enjoys playing in the tub while you soak in a warm bath.
- *Pets*: A dog or cat is often high on the list of expert recommendations for people on the spectrum. Petting, cuddling, or playing quietly with the family pet can be a way to spend time with your child while you de-escalate.
- *Special interests*: If you have a special interest that calms you, perhaps you can find a way to include your toddler. Children are naturally curious. If your special interest is age appropriate (trains: yes, poker: no), you might be

able to convince your toddler to watch videos, help with projects, look at books, sort materials, or just listen to you tell stories about it.

- *Walking*: If you have a quiet place to walk, exercise combined with fresh air and sunshine can be a good way to de-stress for you and an instant sleep-inducer for your little one.
- *Driving*: The same goes for a drive along quiet roads. I remember evenings when Sang and I drove around the neighborhood with Jess napping in her car seat because it was the only way to get an hour of quiet time.

Of course, there is the toddler who screams the minute you put him in his car seat and the Aspie parent who finds driving stressful rather than relaxing. Take some time to think about what activities you find relaxing and then experiment with including your baby and toddler when you're both in a good mood. That way you'll have a trusted list of rescue activities that you can share with your child when you need them.

The Joys of Parenting a Toddler

As difficult as I found being the mom of a newborn, I really enjoyed being the mom of a toddler. Suddenly, this demanding little creature was starting to walk and talk and explore the world around her. She was still demanding and unpredictable and messy, but she was also *fun*.

Discovering the world all over again alongside your child is an incredible experience. And when your little boy or girl develops a fascination with butterflies or dump trucks, you can put your Aspie tendencies to work: visits to the library, field trips to construction sites, collecting things!

As an Aspie, I'd already mastered one of the keys to parenting a toddler: routine. I saw nothing strange about reading *Goodnight Moon* every night before bed, six weeks running. If Jess wanted to watch the same episode of *Blue's Clues* three times in a row, I was the last person who'd think to tell her how great it would be to watch something new once in a while. When she hit that stage where she wanted to take a special toy with her everywhere she went or wear the same sundress every day of the summer, it made perfect sense to me.

When she turned two and started asking "Why?" in response to everything, my natural Aspie response was to explain why the wind blows or why dogs bark. In the end, she not only ended up with vast amounts of esoteric knowledge, she learned that asking "Why?" is a good thing.

On the downside, much of a toddler's social life depends on mom's ability to socialize. Toddlers meet and play with other toddlers at playgroups, the park, and other "Mom and me" events. My inclination toward avoiding social interaction made the neighborhood "Mom and me" playgroup unappealing. But I also knew that Jess needed to play with other toddlers. She wasn't in daycare, so until she was old enough for preschool, it was up to me to make that happen.

Off we went to learn how to finger paint and make macaroni necklaces. The thing about these playgroups is that the moms are there as much to make friends for themselves as they are to socialize their children. I accepted exactly one play date invitation from another mom. It wasn't a disaster exactly, but it was a classic case of wrong planet syndrome. The other mom and I had little in common and I didn't have the social skills to bridge the gap.

Looking back, I realize that we could have spent the hour talking about our toddlers. Faced with this situation now, I would have used the drive to her house thinking up suitable small talk questions. I also know now that "Yes" and "No" are conversation killers, even when they're accurate answers. When she asked me if I liked the playgroup, she didn't want a literal yes or no answer. She was trying to elicit information to continue the conversation. A more suitable answer than "Yes" would have been, "Jess really enjoys story time. Which activities does Peter like best?"

Jess had a great time playing with her new friend and I toughed it out for her, but that was the first and last play date she went on that required my attendance. Because I wasn't armed with even the rudimentary social skills that I've since developed, I struggled to connect with someone who was reaching out to me and missed the chance at making a friend. Instead I came away thinking that there was something very wrong with me and decided that it would be safer to decline future play dates rather than suffer through the kind of self-doubt I felt for days afterward. I suddenly became "very busy" when the other moms raised even a hint of getting together.

Looking back on times like that, it's easy to regret not knowing that I was autistic. It's tempting to say things would have been different if only I'd known this or done that. But I'm not sure it would have been that different. Today, if I was the mom of a toddler and another mom asked us on a play date, I might be more likely to accept than I was 20 years ago, but I don't think I'd enjoy it the same way a typical mom would.

The difference is, I'm okay with that now.

Out into the World

Thankfully, Jess was soon old enough to go on play dates by herself. It turned out she was good at making friends and didn't need me to engineer friendships for her the way my mom had for me. Not only was this a great relief, seeing her develop her own social network was exciting.

While I'd never been good at making friends, she had a natural instinct for socializing. Maybe that's just her personality or maybe she was compensating for my deficits. While the other kindergartners' moms were arranging play dates for their kids, Jess was on her own. If she didn't go out and find some kids to invite over after school, she wasn't going to have much of a social life. She quickly made friends and that paved the way for the years ahead.

With friends came all sorts of new questions. There's a lot of unfiltered knowledge floating around out there on school buses and playgrounds. As an Aspie, I was probably less shocked than the average mom by some of the questions she came home with. As a result, I think Jess grew to feel comfortable coming to me with questions. My natural tendency toward bluntness combined with my higher than average level of emotional detachment contributed to creating a very open mother–daughter relationship. By high school, it seemed like Jess was willing to ask or tell me everything.

Often, 90 percent of everything would have been more than enough.

As middle school approached, I looked back on my own experience and found myself dreading the coming years on Jess's behalf. Middle school is an awkward time, at best. For many autistic individuals, it is the time when our differences start to become very obvious to ourselves and worse, to our peers.

It turned out that the challenges Jess faced in middle school were entirely different from the ones I'd faced. In some ways, she was better off than I had been, simply by virtue of not being autistic. She didn't struggle with the same types of social difficulties that I had. Instead, she experienced her own adolescent hurts and fears.

This left me feeling a bit confused. I was unprepared for how the milestones of her adolescence would affect me.

Reading the experiences of other autistic parents has shown me that it's not unusual for a child's first school dance, big game, or sleepover party to bring up memories of our own early adolescence that we'd rather forget.

When I felt this happening, I tried to remember that my daughter was a very different child than I had been. She had her own adolescent anxieties and the last thing she needed was for me to impose my issues on her. When a crisis arose, I did my best to listen and try to understand what she was facing. This was a big challenge. First of all, I tend to assume that everyone thinks like I do. Cognitive empathy, or perspective taking, is hard to "fake." I also have a tendency to want to fix stuff when often what my daughter needed in a crisis was compassion, understanding, and reassurance. And love.

I found that asking, "How can I help?" or "Is there something I can do that would make you feel better?" worked well when I didn't know what else to do. Often, I relied on Jess or her dad to lead in an emotional crisis. Sometimes this left me feeling like I was failing at parenting, like I should have intuitively known the right thing to do or say. Isn't that what mothers do? It turns out that all parents struggle when it comes to understanding their adolescent children. Maybe I struggled a bit more than most moms, but I hope I made up for it in other ways.

For example, being raised by an Aspie mom seemed to inoculate Jess against peer pressure to a degree. I've always been obliviously, even proudly, different from my peers. Peer pressure doesn't have a lot of effect when you're used to being on the outside looking in at your peer group. While this wasn't something we ever talked about, I think my attitude rubbed off on Jess in positive ways. She's always been very individualistic and even today she takes the view that if people don't like her for who she is then it's their loss.

WHEN TO SHARE YOUR DIAGNOSIS WITH YOUR CHILD

If you have the benefit of a diagnosis, consider sharing that with your adolescent child. Disclosure is a complicated subject and each family handles it differently. However, most experts agree that a middle school age child is old enough to understand the basics of what ASD is and how it makes you different from the average parent. Middle schoolers are also old enough to be asked to make simple accommodations, like setting limits on the amount of noise they make when having friends over or telling you as concretely as possible what they need or want from you if you're having trouble figuring it out.

Lurching Toward Adulthood

As adolescence dragged on—some days it felt like it would never end—we began to face more serious challenges. The wild mood swings, sarcasm, unpredictability, and sometimes downright meanness of teenagers can be especially hard on autistic parents.

I wasn't the most confident parent to begin with. The arrival of a teenager in the house proved to be especially challenging. Suddenly my little girl had pseudo-adult social skills and quasi-adult social crises. It felt like she was leaping right over me into adulthood and I had little clue how to help her navigate the increasingly complicated waters of her social world.

Fortunately, her dad was there to offer advice and bring down the hammer on the few occasions it was necessary. When I was feeling intimidated or overwhelmed by a house full of teenagers, he was carefully watching for problem behavior and never shy about stepping in to enforce the small number of rules that we had. He became the voice of reason in a crisis and the voice of discipline, allowing me to play good cop to his bad cop until Jess reached college.

Which isn't to say that those teenage years were difficult every step of the way or my Aspie nature didn't give me some distinctive strengths as the parent of a teenager. I may have been little help when it came to shopping for dresses for the school dances, but I was cool-headed enough to teach Jess to drive without getting into a shouting match at every rolling stop and crooked parking job. And the research skills I'd developed pursuing my special interests came in handy for everything from homework help to researching colleges.

Then there was my obvious and very un-mom-like quirkiness. My daughter's friends found it amusing that I would spend hours trying to master the Playstation skateboarding tricks that they taught me or that I didn't care if they wrote all over the wallpaper in her bedroom or shaved someone's head in the garage. More than once I heard the words, "Your mom is cool" whispered as I left the room.

Still, it wasn't always easy having kids, and later teenagers, in the house, especially if the visits were unplanned or didn't have a defined end to them. I spent a lot of evenings on edge because of the general anxiety caused by having extra people in the house, but I learned to put up with as much as I could, because I knew it was important for Jess to be able to invite friends over and have a relatively normal social life.

And Jess instinctively learned that I had my limits. She knew that if I disappeared into my basement office, it meant I needed time away from the noise, even if the "noise" was no more than a few kids chatting while they watched TV. She knew that she needed to clean up after herself if she made a mess, that I needed plenty of warning when she was having friends over, and that visits had to be a reasonable duration. Even without understanding all of my autistic traits and what they meant to our relationship, we managed to develop quite a few accommodations over the years.

Growing up in a household with an Aspie parent is going to be different, whether the parent has a diagnosis or not. For a neurotypical kid like Jess, it was probably confusing at times. In a way, she grew up in a bicultural household, and like many children from multicultural families, she learned to intuitively translate between autistic and neurotypical.

There's some question about how having a parent with Asperger's affects a typical child. I definitely see ways in which my Aspie traits have influenced Jess's behavior. She's told me stories about how friends at college or colleagues at work have pointed out deficiencies in her social skills. Although she's a very empathetic, compassionate person with a high emotional IQ, she occasionally does things that others consider thoughtless.

Recently, she was talking with a friend who was discouraged by his job search progress. Her response was much like mine would have been. "It's a tough job market and you just have to keep at it." When he expressed his frustration at how unsympathetic she was being, she realized that she was saying to him what I would have said to her.

Although she understands the social nuances of empathy, she sometimes chooses not to "play by the rules" because she's seen how a less conventional approach has affected her at key points in her life and she finds some value in it that is probably hard for people raised in typical families to relate to.

She's also related stories to me where she was shocked to find out that other people thought she was being rude—for not sharing a birthday treat, for example. These were instances where she simply didn't think about what the social rule was for that situation. More than one person has attributed these faux pas to her being an only child, but I think it has more to do with my ASD than her lack of siblings.

Having an Aspie parent influences a child in unexpected ways, no matter how hard their parents try to compensate or how socially adept the child seems to be. There are unusual habits and behaviors that every child considers normal, often right up until one family member goes out into the world and discovers otherwise. This is true of all families, but it may be more pronounced in families where one or both parents are on the spectrum.

A partner or spouse with a different set of parenting abilities can go a long way toward helping an autistic parent "mind the gap" when it comes to parenting. My husband is everything I'm not when it comes to social skills. He's naturally compassionate, outgoing, empathetic, and confident. He can walk into a room full of strangers and strike up a conversation with anyone. People gravitate toward him. When it comes to our daughter's social skills, I give him 100 percent of the credit. He modeled behaviors for her that don't come naturally to me and that I've never learned to fake well.

As parents, we haven't always seen eye to eye. There were times when he thought I was being too cold-hearted and there were times when I thought he was being too sentimental. We've had to compromise on some issues and agree to disagree on others. We've both made mistakes. But we've also come to realize that we have our own strengths.

When Jess needs sympathy or relationship advice, she usually talks to her dad. When she needs help filling out forms for a new job or fixing her computer, she calls me. She intuitively worked out what we can each give her as parents long before any of us knew what Asperger's was.

6

Rigid and Routine

As a result of growing up undiagnosed, I've developed a lot of instinctive coping strategies for dealing with the challenges of autism. One of the earliest was a strong reliance on rules, routines, and pattern recognition. In fact, many of the traits that psychologists label rigid and routine behaviors actually feel like coping strategies for me. Adherence to routines. Resistance to change. Reliance on social scripts. Attachment to rules.

Not the healthiest or most productive coping strategies, but when you grow up in a world where so many aspects of daily life are confusing and sometimes frightening, you take what you can get. And what I could get, from a very early age, was patterns.

I can't help noticing patterns, and when a pattern is broken I need to know why. I question, dissect, research, and analyze until I find an answer that satisfies me. Often, the answer is some esoteric bit of information that I'll never have a practical use for.

I know that tigers are solitary animals while lions prefer to live in groups. The last half dollar to be made of mostly silver was the 1964 Kennedy half dollar. The normal human body temperature is not actually 98.6 degrees. The minivan was invented to take advantage of a loophole in CAFE standards.

This is probably one of the reasons that Aspies have a reputation as encyclopedias of obscure information. We're the geeks, the brainiacs, the little professors. I've done more than my share to keep this stereotype alive. I'm a treasure trove of seemingly useless facts and I have a superhuman memory for random bits of information.

But not all of the knowledge I've accumulated is useless. Many of the patterns I've picked up on have helped me form my catalog of rules for social interaction, my "if…then…" rules. *If someone is crying, then they're sad. If someone is sad, then they want a hug. If I give them a hug, then they might feel better.* From childhood I've been building up a database of these if…then… rules, hardcoding them into my brain through repetition.

While I didn't know it at the time, my database grew instinctively with each new experience. I've always been more of an observer than a participant. I watch. I collect data. Patterns emerge. A rule forms. I catalog it. Apply it. Adjust, adapt, reformulate.

Watching is safe. Quiet is safe. This is one of the first rules I learned and it stuck in the way that few have since. If I'm quiet, then I'm not getting scolded. If I don't say anything, then there will be nothing for anyone to make fun of. If I watch carefully enough, I can figure out what the rule is here without having to ask and look stupid.

My rules kept me safe. They created a positive feedback loop, naturally rewarding me for following them and punishing me for deviating from them.

I tried to get other people to see the beauty of my rules, but they had their own complex sets of rules. They seemed reluctant to share them or even to follow them consistently. They liked unpredictability. They didn't always need to know how every minute of the day would unfold to enjoy it.

Over time, my rules boxed me in. There were rules for school, rules for work. Rules for marriage. Rules for motherhood. Stay within established parameters. If you can't find a rule for it, avoid it. Breaking the rules causes dire consequences. So dire that they're unknown.

Slowly, unconsciously, my life narrowed, and narrowed further still. The rules became more of a burden than a support.

Choice receded; rigidity crept in.

A few months before learning about Asperger's, I began to realize that I rely on pattern recognition and rules to navigate social interaction. At the time, I didn't understand that these were coping strategies. I simply thought I had an unusual approach to socializing.

Now I know that many autistic people rely on explicit rules, social scripts, pattern recognition, and lots of practice to make social interaction easier. Seeing my rules for what they were—a tool that I'd instinctively developed to make sense of the world—led me to an important realization: the rules are supposed to serve me, not the other way around.

The rules are malleable. I made them; I can unmake them. And so I began editing my rules database.

Many stayed. They're useful. Necessary. Offer someone a beverage when they visit your house. Leave an empty seat between you and another person on the train. Kiss your husband goodbye when he leaves home in the morning.

Some stayed in spite of their apparent uselessness. They're harmless rules. They give order to life. Always swim an even number of laps. The bowls face to the left in the dishwasher. Dry your hair first after showering. The blue towel is mine.

Bad rules got deleted, though not without a struggle. The house has to be spotless if guests are visiting. Items on the 'to do' list must be finished by the end of the day no matter what. Iced coffee has to come from Dunkin' Donuts.

How did I decide which rules were bad? Using rules, of course:

- If a rule prevents me from making a spontaneous choice then it's too restrictive.
- If a rule negatively impacts someone I love then it's probably doing more harm than good.
- If a rule was created more than five years ago then I may have outgrown it.
- If a rule makes me sad, angry, tired, or anxious then I need to question its origins.

As I shed old rules and thought more intentionally about how I approach difficult situations, new and more useful rules emerged. *Think before you automatically say no to a spontaneous change of plans. There is more than one right way to do something.*

Aware now of my ASD, people gifted me with the rules that I failed to intuit. When you say goodbye, look at the person you're talking to, not the direction you're about to walk away in. If you have something important to say, wait until you're face to face to start the conversation.

Throughout my first year of being autistic, I continued to add, delete, overwrite, reorder, sort, categorize, refine. Rules to make my life easier. Rules to help me struggle less. Rules for order and rules for efficiency. Rules to create structure. Rules for navigation. Rules that need breaking now and then.

Even a rule that says, "Worry less about the rules."

Guided by Routine

Like rules, routines have been a primary coping strategy since I was a child. Without routines, my carefully organized life goes all to hell. The plants don't get watered. The dog may or may not get fed. I forget to shower. I get anxious about what's for lunch before I've even finished breakfast. I spend too many hours happily chasing after this idea or that, forgetting that the rest of the world exists.

In the absence of routines, I just plain forget to do things. I drift. I expend too much energy on the blizzard of little choices that typical people find effortless and Aspies find exhausting, never getting around to the more important stuff.

I become all details and no big picture.

Take breakfast, for example. I find it fascinating that some people (a lot of people?) wake up not knowing what they'll have for breakfast. Presumably they walk into the kitchen or the diner or 7-Eleven and decide on the spot what they'd like. This is an amazing feat of executive function and one that I would find stressful beyond words.

I eat the same thing for breakfast every day. It frees me from having to think about what I'm in the mood for in the context of what we have in the house, the comparative calories and nutritional value of my choices, how much time it would take to prepare each choice, the possibility that I've left some better choice off my list not to mention the fact that I'd have to shop for these choices at some point, thereby having to choose not once but twice.

Instead, I grab a bowl, slice up some fruit, dump in my favorite cereal and pour milk over it. It's simple and it makes me happy and I don't have to use up precious brain resources before the sun is barely over the horizon.

Routines give my life structure. Within my routine, I always know what I need to do next or I at least have a limited number of "preprogrammed choices" to pick from. While this doesn't entirely prevent unwanted surprises, it reduces them to a tolerable level.

If you're not thinking, "Yes, exactly!" at this point, you're probably thinking I'm the most boring, rigid, monotonous person in the history of humankind. Not true! I can be flexible if I have to. There are times when breakfast at home isn't an option. Vacations. Special occasions. Power outages. This used to upset me, but I've learned that being grumpy at breakfast when there are so many delicious things to choose from is not only an example of a nonfunctional attachment to routine but a real drag.

At first I had to do the adult equivalent of a social story: sometimes the restaurant doesn't have the food I want to eat. That's okay. There are a lot of other foods on the menu I can try. Many of them are probably things I would enjoy.

Yes, I felt a bit odd having to repeat this to myself, but over time it worked.

Which isn't to say that I'm routine-free on these magical breakfasts away from home. I can be happy with coffee if the restaurant doesn't have chai. I can enjoy French toast as much as an egg sandwich or a bowl of oatmeal.

You won't catch me spontaneously ordering a mango smoothie or freestyling my way through the make-your-own-omelet choices. I still have a routine for breakfast; it's just different.

I've discovered that it's not routines themselves that are problematic, it's the appropriateness of the routine I choose to run. At home, I need to run the home breakfast routine. When I'm out, I need to run the restaurant breakfast routine. The restaurant breakfast routine has more options. It's not one that I'd want to run every day, but I can do it as needed without the negative consequences I'd face if I had no routine at all.

Routines are a basic survival mechanism. Because autistic people have impaired executive function, planning and decision making can be a big drain on our cognitive resources. Routines keep us from getting bogged down in the little decisions that other people make effortlessly throughout the day.

Sometimes, though, we get so attached to our routines that they turn into the "resistance to change" that is one of the diagnostic criteria for autism. I've come to think of it as my "NO" reflex.

The "NO" Reflex

It's Monday morning and Sang is off from work:

> *Him*: Do you want to go to the diner for breakfast?
>
> *Me*: No.

We never go to the diner on Monday. It's not part of The Plan.

We're hiking through a new trail system:

> *Him*: That trail looks interesting. Let's try it.
>
> *Me*: I think we should stick to the route I planned.

I don't even consider whether the other trail might be more interesting. It's not in The Plan.

We're driving home from a quick trip to the mall on Sunday afternoon:

> *Him*: Let's go to the movies!
>
> *Me*: …

That's the sound of my head exploding. Sang is spontaneous. I'm not. He can decide on a whim to go to the movies. He'll drive to the theater, choose a movie that looks decent and is playing soonish, and buy a ticket. Then he'll find a way to kill time until the movie starts. And he might enjoy the movie or be a little bored or end up thinking it sucks, but he'll have a good time regardless.

I don't understand this. At all.

A movie is not part of my daily routine. It requires contingency planning. It raises many many questions that have to be answered before A Plan can be put into place. What will I see? When? Where? Can I get there in time? Will I have to wait? Will I be early enough to get The Right Seat? Do I want popcorn? How long will the movie run? Should I eat before? After? Where? How much time will *that* require?

And my response to all of these questions?

"NO!"

"Do not want."

"Too hard."

"Let's go home and sit quietly and think about maybe going to the movies tomorrow. When we have A Plan."

Yes, that's much better.

I have a very strong NO reflex.

Do I want to do something that isn't part of The Plan? NO.

Do I want to unexpectedly deviate from the schedule? Serendipitously try something new? Alter, vary, or disrupt my routine at the last minute? NO, NO, and NO.

With adequate warning, I manage change pretty well. I vary my schedule, go new places, and try new things without excess trepidation. I need enough lead time so I can mentally prepare myself but once I have a contingency plan, all systems are go.

Without enough warning, however, my instinctive response to anything not in The Plan is NO. Often an emphatic and even angry NO. Yes, unplanned change makes me irrationally angry.

I don't stop to consider whether the change might be better than what I've planned. I don't weigh the pros and cons. I'm not easily persuaded. In fact, the more you try to persuade me, the more panicked I'll start to feel.

And the worst part of this NO reflex is that the change often *is* better.

One antidote to the NO reflex is purposefully making an effort to "be okay" with things.

When someone asks me to do something unexpectedly, I momentarily shush the NO reflex. I let my initial panic at this unexpected request subside, then I try to consider the options objectively.

Breakfast at the diner on a Monday?

> *Evidence in favor*: Spending time with my husband, delicious food, a relaxing start to the week, variety can be refreshing.
>
> *Evidence against*: Cuts into my planned work time, higher fat/sugar breakfast might temporarily affect my mood, there may be some sensory overload to deal with.

As much as I'm tempted to, I don't allow myself to include "Not in The Plan" as evidence against anything. I remind myself that I can be okay with doing something different. I don't have to feel uncomfortable with an out-of-the-ordinary event.

I'll admit, this doesn't always work. Often I'm 80 percent okay and 20 percent uncomfortable. But that's better than not going and beating myself up about it, which is also a strong reflex. It's not like I enjoy raining on everyone's parade. The other option—the one I used to force myself into—was reluctantly going and being 100 percent uncomfortable. Given how unhealthy both of my previous responses were, 20 percent uncomfortable looks pretty good.

I'm not ready for any unplanned trips to the movies, but I'm happy with the day-to-day decisions I make lately that aren't an automatic NO. Sometimes I say yes and sometimes I say no. Each response is a conscious, mindful decision, not a reflexive reaction.

Balancing out my NO reflex with my need for routine is a work in progress. I'm such a creature of habit. It doesn't help that my brain seems to get "stuck" on things so easily.

Persever...what?

Perseveration is a tricky concept. Basically, it means getting stuck on something—an idea, word, phrase, or activity. Technically, perseveration is a repeated response that occurs in the absence of a stimulus. Here's a quick example:

Restaurant hostess: How are you today?

Me: Two!

Hostess: Great!

I was expecting the hostess to ask, "How many?" not "How are you?" Because I'd already rehearsed the answer to the anticipated question (the stimulus) in my head, when the stimulus changed—the actual question was different from the rehearsed question—I couldn't shift my response to something appropriate. I heard the words, "How are you?" but by the time I processed the question, my brain had already pulled the trigger on "Two!"

That's perseveration in action.

Perseveration can take other forms as well:

- asking the same question over and over
- repeatedly going over a minor detail in your head
- struggling to shift topics in a conversation when your partner brings up a new subject
- collecting or memorizing large amounts of "useless" information.

Perseveration can also take the form of infodumping or monologuing. Most autistic people have deep knowledge of certain subjects, we're passionate about our knowledge, and we want to share. Sometimes that desire to share can get out of hand and we find ourselves monologuing or infodumping.

Personally, I'm more likely to infodump when I'm nervous. Falling back on a subject I know is an easy way to keep a conversation going and, honestly, talking about a familiar topic is comforting in stressful social situations. Unfortunately, most people don't want a 30-minute lecture on the nuances of clicker training or the place of women in the Chosun Dynasty. Infodumping is not conversation.

Just because I'm excited about a subject doesn't mean other people care about it. This is where perspective taking enters the picture. Perspective taking means being able to perceive another person's thoughts, feelings, or motivations. Autistic people are often described as being unable to take another person's perspective, as if we're completely oblivious to the fact that other people even have thoughts or feelings.

That's an exaggeration. Most autistic people are aware of the fact that other people are independent beings with their own thoughts and feelings. But we do struggle at times with seeing the world through the eyes of a friend, family member, or conversation partner. When we infodump, we assume that the other person loves our special interest as much as we do.

Because, really, how can they not be interested in our special interests? I'm kidding, of course, but like most Aspies, I take my special interests seriously.

What's so Special about a Special Interest?

In diagnostic terms, a special interest is an "interest that is abnormal in intensity or focus."

You'll notice there are two parts to that criterion: intensity or focus. A special interest can be an intense interest in a broad subject (architecture) or a narrowly focused interest (mid-12th century Cistercian monasteries). Generally, narrowly focused interests are also intense, but a special interest doesn't have to be stereotypically narrow to qualify.

A partial list of my special interests, starting in childhood:

- Barbies
- construction toys (Lego®, Lincoln Logs, Tinkertoy)
- text (reading, writing, words, found text, *Roget's Thesaurus*)
- stamps
- coins
- *The Guinness Book of World Records*
- baseball cards
- sewing (making my own clothes)
- the stock market
- *M*A*S*H* (TV show)
- The Doors
- Star Trek
- martial arts
- human detritus (abandoned places, found objects, discarded things, cemeteries)
- Zen Buddhism
- dog training
- astronomy, especially Messier objects

- the Choson Dynasty
- Shamanism
- national parks
- running
- autism (!)

You can look at that list and think, "But everyone has hobbies, what's so special about yours?" Like much of what differentiates an autistic trait from a simple personality quirk, the answer is the degree to which the trait is present.

For example, when I took up running, I didn't just go out and jog a few times a week. I read books about training for marathons. I found workout plans online and joined a training site to get personalized drills. I learned about fartlek and track workouts and running technique. I signed up for road races. Ten years later, I spend more on running clothes and shoes than on everyday clothes. I use a heart rate monitor and a distance tracker to record my workouts. If I go on vacation, I pack all of my running stuff. I don't just like to run occasionally; running is an integral part of my life.

That's a key differentiator between a run-of-the-mill hobby and an autistic special interest. Spending time engaged in a special interest fulfills a specific need. It's more than just a pleasant way to pass the time. Indulging in a special interest is a way to mentally recharge. It's comforting. It allows me to completely immerse myself in something that intensely interests me while tuning out the rest of the world.

WHEN SPECIAL INTERESTS GO WRONG

The danger in special interests is that they can become consuming. They can take over every conversation, every free minute of the day, every thought. They can be a refuge or a hiding place.

There are days when I'm so engrossed in writing or work (I've made one of my special interests into a career) that I'll happily spend 8 or 10 or 12 hours at the computer. I put dinner on the stove and then forget about it until I smell it burning. The sun sets and hours later I realize the house is pitch dark. If the dog didn't nudge my elbow when it was time for her to go out or be fed, I would temporarily forget that she existed.

Clearly this can be a problem.

Another problem can arise if the object of a special interest is socially unacceptable. When my husband read my list of special interests, he jokingly added himself to it. He was being funny, but sometimes Aspies do take on another person as a special interest. If that person is a celebrity, the Aspie can safely spend hours learning about and admiring that person from afar. But if the person is someone in the Aspie's life, the special interest may be expressed as unwanted attention, harassment, or stalking.

While most special interests are innocuous, if an interest involves behavior that is illegal, taboo, or a threat to your or someone else's health or wellbeing, it may be necessary to seek help in redirecting your attention to a safer alternative.

Nonautistic people often talk about special interests as if they're simply really intense hobbies that we pick up by choice. Among the reasons I've seen suggested for autistic individuals' pursuit of special interests are:

- a need for organization or sameness
- a need to focus on something
- a way to take up all that time left over from not socializing
- a compulsion

- a way to escape reality
- a way to gain emotional satisfaction that we don't get from people.

None of these feels like a complete answer to me. Special interests can certainly be an escape, a compulsion, or a way to fill up time, but there is an element of serendipity to special interests that makes the experience of finding a new passion much like falling in love. Special interests tend to find us, rather than the other way around. I have no idea what has drawn me to many of my special interests over the years. Most are things that I have an intense but inexplicable fascination with.

Take abandoned places. I can't explain what the lure is, but I can spend hours roaming an old townsite or quarry. Like writing, reading, and martial arts, my interest in abandoned places and things has been with me since childhood. But other interests have come and gone over the years. A special interest often arises suddenly, becomes intense for a period (months or years), then disappears just as quickly. My collecting-related interests from childhood were like that. I would spend hours organizing, sorting, and rearranging my coins, stamps, and baseball cards. I'd talk my parents into driving me to collectors' shows, my tattered value guide tucked under my arm, bouncing with excitement at the prospect of filling a hole in one of my collections.

Then, when my interest in one of my collections suddenly dried up, I'd pack my binders and reference books and collecting paraphernalia away in the closet where they'd sit collecting dust while I spent hours comparing annual editions of the *Guinness Book of World Records* to see which records had changed or clipping articles about *M*A*S*H* from magazines so I could add them to my scrapbook.

HOW MUCH IS TOO MUCH?

Special interests are important to most Aspies' happiness and perhaps to our mental health. If I go through a period where I can't engage in my special interests, I get agitated and spend a lot of time thinking about what I'd like to be doing. For me, and for a lot of Aspies, a special interest is our preferred way of de-stressing, recharging, and just plain enjoying ourselves.

But like any good thing, it's possible to overdo it and veer into unhealthy territory. I think it's safe to say that a special interest has become too consuming when it keeps you from taking care of daily responsibilities (school, work, hygiene), negatively impacts your health (lack of sleep, poor eating habits), or has a significant negative impact on loved ones (limited social contact, financial burden).

However, there is one case where you get to pursue your special interest all day, five days a week, and society gives you an approving thumbs up: when you turn a special interest into a career. Suddenly, you're no longer a geek who knows too much about C++ programming, production switchers, or 18th century fashion. You're a computer programmer, an audio equipment repair technician, or a museum curator. Big difference, right?

I've been lucky enough to do this twice, making it perfectly acceptable to dedicate most of my waking hours to a favorite subject. I've read and heard about a lot of Aspies who've done the same with their lifelong special interests. It's certainly not possible for everyone with Asperger's to turn a special interest into a job or career, but when it does work out that way, you get to be one of those lucky people who earns a living doing what you love.

7

Sensory Seeking and Sensitivities

I have difficulty *resting* when I'm at rest.

My body was born to be in motion. I slouch. I splay. I pin one foot under the other. I pull one knee up, then two, hugging my shins with a hand or arm. I sit on my foot, ankle, or calf. I sit cross-legged, even on chairs. I put my elbows on the table, lean my head or chin on my hand, interlace my hands on top of my head. I perch on the edge of my chair, turn sideways, tangle my feet in the legs of nearby furniture.

These constant shifts in position orient my body to my surroundings. Without a steady stream of proprioceptive feedback, I feel disoriented and disconnected from my body. Confused. Physically disorganized.

It's not that I *can't* sit like a proper adult. I often start out sitting with both feet on the ground, arms relaxed at my side. In fact, in unfamiliar social situations, I make a conscious effort to sit properly. Because I'm not four years old. I'm an adult—often an adult in a situation where I'm expected to look professional—and adults expect other adults to know how to sit in a chair.

Then my internal clock starts ticking and my body will grow more and more tense as I work to maintain a polite, socially acceptable posture. Soon I'll start covertly rubbing something between my fingers or twisting my hand in my pants leg as a way to counterbalance the tension that's building up while I force myself to be still.

Stimming as Sensory Regulation

Those little movements that erupt when I have to be still are known as stimming. It is generally believed that stimming has a function related to sensory input. Most autistic people say that they finding stimming to have a regulatory function—stimulating at times, calming at other times.

This is definitely true for me. I stim when I'm anxious. I stim when I'm thinking. I stim when my senses are overloaded. I stim when I'm happy. Stimming is a way of regulating my body and mind. It calms me when I'm over-stimulated and reconnects me with myself when I'm under-stimulated. Most of the time, stimming is a subconscious activity; I don't even notice that I'm doing it. When I am conscious of it, it feels good: comforting, calming, soothing, fulfilling.

STIMMING COMES IN MANY FORMS

Although stimming often takes the form of movements like rocking, flapping, spinning, or bouncing, there are many other types of stims including:

- watching a moving object or pattern
- smelling preferred smells
- touching or rubbing objects, surfaces, or textures
- making or repeating sounds, words or phrases silently in your head or out loud
- creating pain or pressure, such as by lip biting, skin picking, head banging, or lying on your arms
- manipulating a stim toy or object with your fingers or hand
- engaging in a repetitive task, either manually or intellectually (stacking or sorting objects, doodling, shuffling cards, factoring large numbers).

As a child, my stims were more obvious than they are today: bouncing, rocking, twitching, flapping, hopping. Four decades later, my stimming is often discreet. You'd have to be watching closely to notice that I'm rubbing my thumbs over the spacebar on my keyboard when I stop typing. Or that I'm fidgeting with a bottle cap under the table at a restaurant or playing with my hair while driving or folding and unfolding a piece of paper while I wait in the bank.

Stimming is so much a part of who I am that I when first read about autistic traits, I completely denied that I stim. It was only when I started to read the writing of other autistic adults that I discovered how varied and subtle stimming can be. My stims had essentially gone undercover as I'd grown older.

Not only did I learn to stim with my hand in my pocket or beneath the table, but I found ways to create sensory input without moving at all. Often, the positions I find most comfortable—the ones that serve the same sensory function as stimming movements—involve pressure. I frequently sit with one part of my body pinned, pressed, squeezed, or wedged against or under something—either another body part or a piece of furniture.

This deliberate pressure creates feedback that grounds my body physically. Pressure equals organization. It reminds me of where my body is in space and makes me feel safe.

Sensory Seeking Gone Wild

In addition to craving pressure, I also crave motion.

The summer before seventh grade I went to an amusement park with my cousins. It was my first time in a *real* amusement park with real rides and I was...terrified. I felt sick to my stomach just looking at the rides. But my cousins, who had been to the park many times, took me by the hands and made a beeline straight for a ride called "Strawberry Fields." My memory of sitting between them, waiting for the ride to start is as clear as if it happened yesterday. I can hear the scratchy version of "Lucy in the Sky with Diamonds" playing on the loudspeakers above us, feel the greasy vinyl of the safety bar beneath my sweaty palms, and practically taste my fear as my heart galloped in my chest.

And then we started to move, slowly at first, gaining speed until the wind was whipping my hair across my face and the three of us were pressed in a bone-crunching heap against the outside of the car and I was screaming right along with everyone else through 90 seconds of pure, unadulterated joy.

When the ride stopped, all I could think was, "Let's do that again!" And again and again and again.

I'd discovered one of my favorite sensory experiences: going fast. The speed was exhilarating. I rode everything in the park. The faster it went, the more I liked it. Spinning, falling, dipping, swinging—I had no idea why I liked the intense physical sensations that the rides created, but I did.

Now that I know about sensory-seeking behavior, my sudden intense love of amusement park rides makes sense. Autistic people are sensory seekers. We have a strong need for intense sensory input and will deliberately seek out or create sensory experiences to satisfy that need.

Like stimming, sensory seeking is often described as a way to either stimulate an under-stimulated nervous system or calm an over-stimulated system. Much of my childhood play was sensory seeking in disguise. Some of my favorite activities as a kid were:

- going as fast as I could down big hills on my bike, roller skates, or sled
- jumping or diving off the high board
- hanging upside down and doing somersaults on the monkey bars

- jumping on the bed (broke my jaw doing this)
- bouncing on a trampoline or hippity hop
- sit 'n' spin!
- climbing trees to hang upside down from the branches or jump to the ground
- running into the padded gymnasium wall and bouncing off
- zipping my arms into my coat and playing crash dummies with a friend (this never ended well)
- lying underneath my beanbag chair while watching TV
- swinging as high as I could on the swings, then leaping off.

As a teenager I took up martial arts, primarily for self-defense, but I discovered that I liked the contact that sparring involves. Getting hit while padded up with gear creates a very tangible kind of physical feedback. So does punching a heavy bag or kicking a hand target hundreds of times in a row.

Although that may sound masochistic, it's not. I don't seek out pain. Although I often engage in activities that have a risk of injury and pain, what I'm looking for is a benign physical sensation—one of pressure or contact or movement—not pain.

There is sometimes a belief that people who engage in sensory-seeking activities like headbanging, slamming into objects or biting themselves are doing it because pain is the desired outcome. That may be true for some, but for others those activities don't hurt, either due to pain hyposensitivity or an ability to regulate the level of contact in a way that keeps it below their pain threshold.

64 Flavors of Sensory Seeking

While I'm primarily a proprioceptive and vestibular sensory seeker, everyone's sensory-seeking preferences are different. Some common examples of sensory-seeking experiences by category:

- *Tactile*: seeking touch from others; touching objects, textures, or surfaces (either certain types or everything).
- *Visual*: seeking visual patterns, moving objects, specific colors, or shapes.
- *Oral*: seeking food or nonfood objects to taste, chew or suck on; seeking specific sensations like crunchy, spicy, or minty.
- *Olfactory*: seeking specific preferred smells; smelling everything.
- *Vestibular*: spinning, rocking, being upside down; seeking specific head or body positions; jumping from heights; seeking intense speed or movement.
- *Auditory*: seeking loud, repetitive, or specific types of noises; making sounds because they're pleasing.
- *Interoceptive*: seeking bodily sensations like hunger, thirst, urgency to use the bathroom, fatigue.
- *Proprioceptive*: seeking physical contact, crashing into things, stretching, pressure, sound resonance.

What drives us to seek out our preferred sensory inputs? There are a few common theories:

- *Regulatory*: Sensory seeking soothes an overloaded brain. It's common for sensory-seeking behaviors to increase during times of stress, anxiety, pain, or sensory overload. Sensory seeking can also be stimulating, providing us with needed input during periods when our brain is underactive.

- *Connection*: Sensory input can help us connect our mind and body by creating distinct physical sensations in specific areas of the body. It can also help connect the body to the environment in tangible ways. Without touch, pressure, and movement, some of us easily get disconnected from our physical selves.
- *Organization*: Some types of sensory input can help us feel mentally and physically organized and integrated. For example, many people find that using a weighted lap pad helps them focus better on difficult school or work tasks.

Stimming and sensory-seeking activities are a fundamental aspect of being autistic. They fulfill very basic needs—regulation, comfort, organization. Sadly, many of the ways that we satisfy our sensory-seeking urges are considered socially unacceptable. Too many autistic adults have told me that they've "lost" their favorite childhood stims because they were punished or chastised for flapping, rocking, or other movements as children.

About six months after getting diagnosed, I was shocked one day to wake up from a dream in which I flapped my hands. Before that night, I was never aware of myself stimming in a dream and even more curiously, I hadn't flapped since early childhood. From watching old home movies, I know that I flapped as a toddler and preschooler. I'm not sure when I lost my flap but my best guess is very early in elementary school.

The truly incredible part of the dream was that in the moment when I flapped, I was flooded with the sensation of being connected to my original self. It felt like a wormhole to the past opened up and for the briefest moment I was able to experience myself as a very young child, before I learned all of the rules and social constructs that created the boundaries of my adult persona.

It was around that time that I began to feel like I was slowly rediscovering my original autistic self.

Part of that rediscovery was tuning in to my urge to stim and setting it free. Too many years of reflexively quieting my body, of squeezing my stims down to their least noticeable versions, had disconnected me from myself in an essential way.

Slowly, the stims of my childhood are coming back. The day after I had that dream, as I was waiting for pasta to cook, I found myself twirling in the kitchen and instead of stopping, I let myself enjoy it. I kicked out my foot and made a full spin to the right, then kicked out my other foot and twirled to the left. I did it again and again and soon I found myself laughing out loud.

Twirling around in the kitchen felt good. It felt right.

In the process of unlearning my habit of minimizing my stims, I feel like I'm reintegrating parts of myself that have been disconnected for a very long time. It's a slow process and one that goes against the social conditioning we learn as part of learning to pass for "normal." But it's also an essential part of becoming my autistic self.

Autistic bodies have very specific sensory needs, which are different from those of typical bodies. Not only do we require different types of input to balance our sensory systems, we also perceive sensory input differently.

Sensory Sensitivities

The opposite side of sensory seeking is sensory sensitivities. Autistic people have difficulty filtering or modulating sensory input, making certain types of sensory information intolerable. The exact same sensory input might have no effect on a typical person because their sensory system filters or modulates the input down to a tolerable level.

Sensory overload has both emotional and physical consequences. Too much sensory input can cause anxiety, fear, panic, and a feeling of helplessness, often leading to a shutdown or meltdown. Physically, overload can cause everything from queasiness to unbearable pain.

There are ways to reduce the impact of environmental sensory triggers. At home or in environments we frequent daily, modifying our surroundings to remove or reduce triggers is essential. When visiting public places, many autistic people carry a sensory rescue kit containing things like sunglasses, noise-cancelling headphones and stim toys.

Most autistic individuals have sensory sensitivities, but the type and intensity vary greatly from person to person. It's common to have one or two senses that are especially sensitive while others are moderately sensitive.

LIGHT SENSITIVITIES

The most common form of light sensitivity is to fluorescent lights. Not only do fluorescent lights emit a low-pitched hum, they tend to flicker in intensity. The light they give off can be harsh and overly intense. Often autistic people will find it hard to concentrate in a room lit with fluorescent lighting. Unfortunately, most classrooms, offices, workplaces, and stores have fluorescent lighting, making it hard to avoid.

Ideally, changing the light source to a cooler, less intense type of light or taking advantage of natural light sources is the best way to reduce the effects of light sensitivities. When this isn't possible, sometimes wearing sunglasses indoors is helpful. My light sensitivities are moderate so I've made only a few adaptations: wearing sunglasses outdoors (especially for driving), choosing living and work spaces with as much natural light as possible to eliminate the need for artificial light sources during the day, and watching television with a soft light on in the room to reduce the harshness of the screen.

Light sensitivities can be very serious. Visual overload, especially from bright or flickering light sources, can cause nausea, headache, pain in the eyes, dizziness, disorientation, and even seizures.

SENSITIVITY TO SOUND

I've stopped asking people, "Do you hear that?" when I pick up on up some unexplained faint sound. The answer is inevitably "No." Autistic people tend to have very sensitive hearing. I not only hear the people in the apartment upstairs talking, I can make out entire conversations. In restaurants, my brain automatically tracks conversations at all of the nearby tables, making it a challenge to concentrate on what's being said at my own table.

Not only does our hearing seem to be overly sensitive, we have difficulty turning it off. What most people's brains filter out as useless background noise, autistic brains register in a constant stream of incoming auditory data that is impossible to ignore. It's not like I want to hear the person sitting next to me in the library chewing gum and typing and breathing, but I can't *not* hear it.

This barrage of sound often results in sensory overload in public places, especially crowded public places like stores, restaurants, or public transit. It can also make it difficult to follow conversations or make out speech in environments with a lot of background noise. I'm constantly having to ask strangers to repeat themselves. It was only after learning about auditory processing difficulties that I realized I also use lipreading to augment my hearing when it comes to understanding spoken language. If I can't see a person's mouth, I'm much more likely to have to ask them to repeat something.

Many autistic people find that using noise-cancelling headphones or earbuds playing music helps to reduce the risk of sound overload in public. This strategy can also help minimize an overdeveloped startle reflex, which is common in people with noise sensitivities. I startle at the slightest provocation. Even my husband unexpectedly walking into a room and asking me a question at normal volume can make me jump in my chair and yelp in surprise. Loud sounds, on the other hand, not only provoke a startle reflex, they can be painful and bring on many of the same physical symptoms as light sensitivities.

SENSITIVITY TO SMELL AND TASTE

Smell and taste are controlled by chemical receptors on the tongue (taste) and in the nose (smell and taste). Often someone who has sensitivities in one area also has sensitivities in the other because when it comes to food, our senses of taste and smell are closely linked. It's hard to imagine eating foods that smell repulsive. Often, just the smell of a particular food being prepared will trigger a gag reflex in someone with taste and smell sensitivities.

Many autistic children and adults eat a restricted diet because they find so many foods intolerable. For some, strong flavors or smells are triggers, while for others specific categories such as citrus, tomato, or mint trigger sensitivities. These types of sensitivities are very hard to overcome because the physical response to triggering tastes and smells can be overpowering, making it physically impossible to be near the food, let alone eat it. Fortunately, it's possible to create nutritious meals while sticking to a bland or restricted diet if necessary.

Beyond food sensitivities, smell sensitivities can extend to nearly anything in our daily environment. Some people have very specific smell triggers like wet animal fur or deodorant. Others are sensitive to strong smells, such as perfume, personal grooming products, detergents, or air fresheners. Many categories of smell sensitivities can be hard to avoid in public places because they are both common and hard to anticipate. Carrying a familiar object with a pleasing smell, such as a handkerchief scented with vanilla or lavender, is a good emergency defense against unexpected triggering scents.

TACTILE SENSITIVITIES

Tactile sensitivities, often called tactile defensiveness, are characterized by a negative reaction to a tactile stimulus that is generally considered nonirritating by most people. The nonirritating tactile stimuli that irritate me include: seams (especially in socks), tags, ruffles, lace, synthetics, wool, *tags*, tight/high waists, exposed elastics, stitching that I can feel against my skin, collars that are too high, collars that are too open, TAGS, shirts that are too loose or formless, and sleeves that are anything other than standard short- or long-sleeve length.

My tactile sensitivities have also led to dozens of little quirks, most of which started in childhood. I've never liked the feeling of water spraying on my face (oddly, I'm fine with having my face underwater). If I'm eating something messy with my fingers, I clean them on a napkin between every bite. When my skin gets too cold, it itches worse than a case of poison ivy. If someone kisses me on the cheek, I immediately wipe the little wet spot from my face.

Tactile defensiveness is believed to be caused by overly sensitive light touch receptors in the skin. We also have deep touch receptors, which function differently and seem less likely to be affected by tactile sensitivities. This is why autistic people are often hypersensitive to light touch but crave and seek out deep pressure touch. Occupational therapists recommend sensory tools like weighted blankets and lap pads to help people with tactile sensitivities get the pressure they crave. Tight hugs and wedging our bodies into tight spaces are other ways of getting pressure.

THE IMPACT OF SENSORY SENSITIVITIES ON INTIMACY

Sensory sensitivities can have a big impact on an intimate relationship.

Light touching—the kind often associated with seduction and sensuality—makes many autistic people tense up and pull away due to overstimulation. For years, my aversion to sensual touching was a source of frustration. My husband didn't understand why I was randomly rejecting him. And it wasn't a polite, "Not tonight, dear, I have a headache" rejection. It was a very literal "Don't touch me," often muttered as I shoved his hand away. Unfortunately, I had no explanation for why I disliked being touched at certain times or in specific ways.

Now that I understand touch sensitivity, we've made adaptations. I don't think I'll ever enjoy light touching and we've both accepted that. Fortunately, many types of sexual touching and contact fall into the realm of deep pressure, meaning that it's possible to have a rewarding sex life even if you suffer from tactile defensiveness. It may require some patience and communication, as well as a bit of research and experimenting, but it's definitely possible.

Other sensory sensitivities can wreak havoc in the bedroom as well. Sensitivities to taste, smell, or texture can make certain sexual activities unpleasant or even intolerable.

A few things to keep in mind as you explore this area with your partner:

- *Communicate.* Talk about what feels good and what is uncomfortable. In particular, talk about types of touch or activities that need to be completely off limits.
- *Respect sensory limits.* Don't assume that a partner with sensory sensitivities just needs to "get used" to a certain kind of touch, smell, or taste. That may not be possible.
- *Be flexible.* There are many ways to enjoy sex, some of which might require creativity or open-mindedness.
- *Don't take it personally.* If a partner with sensory sensitivities doesn't like certain kinds of touching, it probably has nothing to do with how well the other partner is doing it.
- *Be prepared for things to change.* What is okay at one point in time might not be okay at another. Keep the lines of communication open.

Many autistic people are sensitive to food textures, which is a form of tactile sensitivity. In particular, foods that are slippery, slimy, gooey, mushy, or fibrous are common triggers. Food texture sensitivities can lead to eating a limited diet. Some autistic adults have found creative ways to overcome texture sensitivities, including cooking foods less or not at all and chopping up foods into very small pieces to minimize the amount of texture that is detectable in the mouth.

OTHER COPING STRATEGIES

Some occupational therapists believe that most children on the spectrum outgrow sensory sensitivities. Perhaps the children who get occupational therapy in childhood do. I haven't, and judging from the postings on ASD forums, neither have many other adults. Fortunately, there are ways to work around or mitigate sensitivities, and when that isn't possible, sometimes the best option is to simply avoid triggers as much as possible.

One strategy that isn't recommended is attempting to suppress a reaction to sensory overload. In the short term, ignoring sensory overload often leads to a shutdown or meltdown (depending on the person). In the long term, it can lead to physical illness: headaches/migraines, fever, digestive system upset, body aches/stiffness, excessive sleeping or inability to sleep, malfunctioning of the body's temperature regulation system, loss of appetite, or fainting/passing out. If you have sensory sensitivities, "toughing out" situations or trying to suppress your body's natural reaction is unhealthy, both physically and mentally.

8

The Autistic Body

One of the most surprising things I've learned about being autistic is how much it affects my body. Initially, I thought autism was purely a social disorder—that it only affected the way I see the world or how I think. Gradually, as I learned more about ASD, I discovered that being autistic has a significant impact on how my body functions. Sensory seeking and sensory sensitivities are a big part of this but so are some lesser-known aspects of being autistic.

For example, Aspies are notoriously clumsy and I'm no exception. I'm forever tripping over stuff, bumping into stuff, dropping stuff, breaking stuff. Seriously, if you like your stuff, keep me away from it.

I've broken an entire kitchen's worth of glassware in my lifetime. In the first month of owning a new blender, I broke the glass pitcher not once, but twice. You'd think I would have learned the first time not to put it down so forcefully on the granite counter. After the second one shattered, I downgraded to a plastic pitcher because a blender is not worth that kind of emotional trauma.

When I set out to research why people on the spectrum tend to be uncoordinated, I quickly ran into a confusing mess of theories: motor planning deficit, motor development delay, motor timing impairment, problems with initiation or inhibition, imitation and praxis impairments, deficient postural control, under-reliance on feedforward control. There are also a handful of other conditions that muddy the waters further: apraxia, ataxia, hypotonia, dysgraphia, dyscalculia, dyskinesia...

Overwhelmed by the sheer number of possible explanations, I decided to focus on the most important questions: what does this mean in my daily life and what can I do about it?

Most of the experts agree that:

- some level of gross and fine motor impairment is nearly universal in people on the spectrum
- the cause of motor development delay in autism is unknown
- motor impairments may improve somewhat with age, but generally persist into adulthood.

In other words, if you're autistic, you're probably somewhat clumsy and you probably always will be, but no one really knows why. While fine and gross motor impairments are not part of the official diagnostic criteria for ASD, autistic children routinely receive occupational therapy to improve their fine motor coordination, balance, and posture. The uncoordinated Aspie isn't just a stereotype. Impaired motor function is real and pervasive and it affects our ability to do everything from writing our names legibly to playing sports.

Unfortunately, I never got the memo regarding unathletic Aspies. All my life I've loved sports and being physically active. Loving sports, in my case, isn't the same as being good at sports, but I've never let that stop me.

Though my parents didn't know I had Asperger's they did know that I was uncoordinated. One of their nicknames for me was "Grace"—as in "Careful there, Grace" and "That's our daughter, Grace." This is funnier when you're the one saying it than when you're the one tripping over an inanimate object.

To help me overcome my lack of coordination, they signed me up for a lot of individual sports: dance, gymnastics, bowling, golf, diving, swimming, karate. They bought me roller skates and ice skates and a bicycle.

All of the childhood sports I enjoyed were things I could do alongside other kids without the intense interaction of typical team sports. I was on a bowling team. Being on a team meant that I took turns with four other kids. The bowling itself was an individual pursuit. Other kids took a turn. I took a turn. I got to add up the scores. I wandered off to watch one of the arcade games. Someone called me back when it was my turn. It was great.

Golf and dance and karate were the same. I did these things alongside other kids but not really with them. There was an appearance of social interaction. The actual amount of interacting I did was minimal and that was fine.

I tried team sports. In middle school, I was on the school softball and basketball teams. It was fun but I wasn't very good at it and spent most of my time sitting on the bench during games. Team sports were confusing and often overwhelming. My basketball coach was always yelling at me to be "more aggressive" but I had no idea what she meant.

There was a lot about basketball that I didn't quite get. Team sports have many variables—the rules, the other team members, the fast pace, the ball (inevitably there's a ball involved). For the typical Aspie, this is a lot to manage. By the time I got to high school, I knew that team sports weren't for me.

But, individual sports! This is where autistic people can shine. When I'm out running on a dirt trail or gliding across the pool, I feel strong and athletic. I feel like I'm graceful and connected to my body. For a short time I forget that I'm the same person who regularly walks into furniture. I've also grown more coordinated over the years. I'll never be a superior athlete—I have to work hard just to be average—

but I think individual sports have a lot to offer for people on the spectrum.

SEVEN REASONS WHY INDIVIDUAL SPORTS ARE A GOOD FIT FOR AUTISTIC INDIVIDUALS

1. *You can progress at your own pace*. Individual sports allow you to measure your progress against yourself. While you might compete against others, most individual sports also encourage "personal bests." Running a new best time for a mile or swimming a personal best for a 400 is as fulfilling as beating an opponent. Maybe more so, because it's an indication that your practice is paying off and you're better at your sport than you were a month ago or a year ago.

2. *You can be part of a team without the pressures of a team sport*. Individual sports can be less stressful than team sports when it comes to having to perform well every time. If you have a bad day as a team player, your actions can impact the whole team negatively. If you have a bad day as a cross-country runner, you might not place well, but one of your fellow runners could still win the race. There are team consequences, but they tend to be less severe.

3. *You can practice by yourself*. This is a huge advantage for people on the spectrum. Because of our motor coordination deficits, we might need a lot more practice than the average person to learn or master a skill. When that skill is something that doesn't require a team or a partner to practice, we can spend hours working on it alone, at our own pace.

4. *You play side by side with others*. Team sports put a big emphasis on bonding with other team members, which can be stressful when you're autistic. Individual sports allow you to play alongside others, interacting as much or as little as you feel comfortable with.

5. *Individual sports tend to be rhythmic, repetitive, and predictable.* And what do we like more than rhythmic, repetitive, predictable movement? Running, cycling, and swimming are like large-scale stims. And you can do them for as long as you like. The more, the better!
6. *Individual sports can burn off a lot of excess energy.* Many individual sports are endurance based. Even moderately vigorous physical activity will burn off excess energy and trigger the release of endorphins, which not only improve your mood but can reduce anxiety and help you sleep better.
7. *Individual sports improve coordination.* All sports improve coordination, but individual sports tend to be more "whole body" sports, requiring you to integrate all of the parts of your body to achieve the best possible result. Think of the type of movement required for swimming breaststroke (continuous, repetitive, predictable movements) versus the type of movement required for playing shortstop (sudden, unpredictable movements in response to a batted ball, interspersed with long periods of activity).

Of all the individual sports I've tried, it's the martial arts that have had the biggest impact on me. When I was in middle school, I asked my parents to sign me up for karate lessons. I wasn't exactly sure what it was about martial arts lessons that fascinated me, but I bugged my mom and dad until they agreed to check into it. Eventually they took me to visit a karate school in a nearby town, but for whatever reason, they didn't enroll me in classes.

Fast-forward a couple of years to freshman year in high school. A different karate school was offering self-defense classes as an after-school activity. The day I saw the announcement, I signed up. It was only once a week and just a few other girls joined, and what I remember most about those first lessons was how disappointing they were. I don't know what I expected. Maybe I'd seen one too many episodes of *Mission Impossible*. Karate chopping bad guys into unconsciousness with a single blow looked surprisingly easy when they did it on TV.

The self-defense moves we learned in the after-school class were more about breaking free from an attacker and running away. Perfectly suitable for 14-year-old girls in need of self-defense. Not nearly enough to satisfy my (by that point) obsessive interest in martial arts.

When the course ended, I found myself begging my parents to let me enroll in classes at the instructor's school. Thankfully, this time it worked out. I was soon sporting a karate uniform and a stiff new white belt.

The school was on the second floor of an old building in a not-so-great neighborhood, as martial arts schools tended to be in those days. Most of the other students were men. There were a few teenage boys, a woman or two and one female part-time instructor, who I found more intimidating than even the toughest-looking guys in the class.

Because the school was small when I first joined, there was one class a night, attended by a mix of new and experienced students. The new students were expected to learn by observing and imitating the higher-ranking members. Which I discovered the hard way, during my very first class, when I decided to "line up" in the front row.

In my excitement, I completely missed the fact that students stood on the mat in rank order, with the highest-ranking black belts in the front row, those with colorful belts in the middle rows and the lowliest white belts at the back. One of the black belts set me straight, as they would so often over the next four years. And he was surprisingly kind about it, considering the fact that I was standing in his spot—the spot where the highest-ranking person in class traditionally stood.

The back row turned out to be pretty comfortable. No one could see all of the mistakes I was making, and there were many. For months, I went left when the rest of the class went right, because the instructor demonstrated movements facing us. Spatial awareness has never been my strong suit. It wasn't unusual to find myself finally getting the hang of a movement, only to have the instructor announce we were moving on to something else. Thankfully, there was lots of repetition from one class to the next and a finite set of skills that a white belt was expected to master.

At home, my parents helped me set up a practice area in our basement. I spent hours down there going over what I was learning in class. The repetition was comforting and the clearly defined goals suited my need for certainty. I knew that if I practiced hard enough, I'd soon be a yellow belt. And an orange belt after that, and then green, and brown, and so on, until I reached the coveted black belt.

It was all very logical and orderly. Unlike my friends playing sports at school, I didn't have to compete with anyone for a place on the team. There were no points to score and no ball to drop. There was just practice. Lots of it.

If I had a question, the senior ranking students were there to help. All I had to do was approach them, bow respectfully and ask my question, making sure to preface it with a deferential "Sir" or "Ma'am." Everything that happened in the school—from where we stood to how we dressed—was very ritualized, which made it easy, predictable, safe. I didn't have to make small talk or find someone who would be my friend. There was a clear social hierarchy and an explicitly defined set of rules for getting help.

There was also an ethical code that was strictly enforced. Courtesy. Integrity. Perseverance. Self-control. Indomitable spirit. We were expected to treat each other—and ourselves—with respect. Hard work was rewarded and there was no room for teasing, bullying, or showing off. For a kid who had spent years getting bullied, who lacked self-esteem and longed for recognition, these rules created a cocoon of safety. And a path to discovering a surprisingly deep well of internal strength.

As I advanced through the ranks, I found myself spending more and more time at the school—often four nights a week—volunteering to help out with the kids' class before mine or staying for an extra practice session after my regular one finished. Adolescence was in full bloom and I was discovering meltdowns—real full-blown autistic meltdowns—for the first time.

Without my noticing, the karate school was becoming a refuge.

We were a motley group. The demographics changed little over the four years I was there, but no one seemed to care that I was a teenage girl. They treated me like one of the guys and that was fine with me. Talking in class was frowned upon. Dating was out of the question. Most importantly, no one invited me to "hang out this weekend," a teenage social interaction that I found increasingly scary as drinking and drugs crept into the equation.

And I got to punch and kick stuff!

Surprisingly, considering how shy and meek I was, hitting stuff was one of the high points of class. There were heavy bags and padded targets, a *makiwara* (traditional rope-covered striking post) and even the occasional geared-up classmate to kick and punch. I realize now why I enjoyed the contact aspect of karate so much. It satisfied my sensory-seeking needs and helped me burn off all the extra energy that was suddenly coursing through my body, thanks to adolescent hormone surges. Autistic adolescence is not a fun time. Martial arts training probably saved me from doing a lot of stupid things with all of the pent-up frustration and confusion I was feeling.

No matter what happened during the school day or over a weekend, I had karate class to look forward to. When I stepped on the mat, everything else disappeared for an hour or two. The intense concentration required to master the moves. The physical exhaustion that came from giving one hundred percent to everything I did in class. The peace I felt as we sat in meditation, my mind settling at last, even for a few minutes.

I still hadn't learned to karate-chop someone unconscious with a single blow, but I'd found what I was looking for. And a whole lot more. Moving up through the ranks, from the back row to the middle row and eventually to the front row, I started to notice that people were coming to me with their questions. The first time someone bowed and addressed me as "ma'am" I felt a little tingle of awe. Someone was looking up to me. Someone wanted advice from me.

And unlike at school, where I often knew the answers to questions when the other kids didn't, at karate class, I wouldn't look like a show-off or a know-it-all for helping someone else out. The higher-ranking students were *expected* to correct the newer students. Slowly, I grew into the role of senior student, occasionally being asked to lead warm-ups or demonstrate a skill in front of the class. My confidence, which had never been very good, started to blossom.

The martial arts were the first thing I was ever really good at. I was good at school, true, but academics came naturally. Karate was something I had to work at, something that I felt like I'd achieved through effort and patience and persistence. And that was a surprisingly rewarding feeling.

I stuck with the martial arts for nearly two decades. First karate, mixed with a little judo, then a lot of taekwondo and some weapon arts. Eventually, my martial arts training was responsible for two careers and finding a husband. While I certainly doubt most people will get that much out of it, I do think martial arts training can be beneficial for many people on the spectrum, especially youngsters.

Unlike that mixed-level class I started out in, most schools now have classes just for beginners, and instructors today are skilled at working with people who have atypical learning styles. In fact, a lot of things in the martial arts world have changed, but the core things that I loved are still there.

Classes are still highly structured and have lots of repetition built into each lesson. Everyone progresses at their own pace. There's no competition for playing time or positions. Yes, you have to interact with others in the class, but that interaction is often structured and a good instructor will make sure that students are paired up with practice partners who are similar in skill level and temperament.

For those of us with motor skill deficits, the repetition of a limited set of movements is a great way to build up coordination and balance, not to mention general body awareness. I can't imagine how clumsy I would be if I hadn't spent all those hours on the mat. Even today, if I take a fall while I'm out running, I instinctively go into the type of rolling fall that I first learned as a teenager.

And finally, there is the sensory-seeking aspect of training. When I taught children's classes, we basically spent the entire 50 minutes in a whirl of running, jumping, falling, throwing, wrestling, shouting, and hitting things, wrapped up with a few minutes of quiet time at the end. Of course the kids were learning new skills in the process, but they were also getting a well-rounded sensory diet. Parents would marvel at how calm their children were after class. Even the kids who never sat still at home made it through our end-of-class meditation sessions without getting fidgety. I didn't know what a sensory diet was at the time, but I did know what I liked most about karate class when I was younger.

I never did learn to drop someone with a single blow and I never figured out what it truly was that first drew me to the martial arts. I suppose it was like any special interest—an inexplicable love affair with something few of my peers even knew existed. When the girls at school asked me why I was "so into that kung fu stuff," my answer was always, "I don't know. I just like it."

It's amazing that "I just like it" was enough to sustain a two-decade-long interest in a pastime that demanded so much commitment, physically and mentally. Although I stopped teaching and training after having major knee surgery in my 30s, the things I learned on the mat have stayed with me. The body awareness. The knowledge that I can physically protect myself if I have to. The ability to calm my mind under pressure. The confidence that comes from being good at something.

Most importantly, I discovered that mindful physical activity is a reliable way to manage my mental and emotional states. Like a lot of autistic adults, I'm prone to bouts of anxiety and depression. When I don't exercise regularly, my moods get out of whack. I get overloaded more easily. I don't sleep as well. I find it more difficult to focus. Even the smallest annoyances feel unbearable.

One of the most difficult periods of my life was the year after I tore a ligament in my knee. Not only had I lost my beloved daily martial arts practice, but I couldn't walk more than a few hundred yards at a time in the months after the reconstructive surgery. I sunk into a deep depression. When I was finally cleared for physical activity, Sang suggested that we take up running.

I thought it sounded like a terrible idea but I was so physically restless and out of shape that I was willing to give it a try. It took months to get to the point where I could run more than ten minutes without needing a walking break, but I stuck with it. Like karate, running turned out to be something I could learn to be good at. It didn't start as an obsession, but it became one. I found myself looking forward to my runs as much as I'd looked forward to being on the mat. Out in the woods, running little-used trails, I started to recapture the joy of challenging my body and mind to the limit.

Eventually, I came to realize that hard physical exercise helps my body balance my moods, burning off the byproducts of stress and anxiety while generating a nice steady flow of positive chemicals. I still have bad moods, but they're less likely to hang around when I'm running, swimming, walking, or hitting the weights at the gym regularly.

I've also discovered that being physically active keeps me connected to my body. When I'm running, I'm acutely aware that my body exists. I feel my muscles working, my heart beating, my lungs expanding. I sense the pavement beneath my feet and the air against my skin. Afterward, the exhaustion that so many people complain about—to me, that's the feeling of being alive.

Insomnia and ASD

While I've known since childhood that I'm not very coordinated, I had no idea that I suffer from insomnia. It was only when I came across an article linking ASD to sleep problems that I recognized my sleep patterns as typical signs of insomnia:

- prolonged sleep latency (time to fall asleep)
- reduced sleep efficiency (decreased ratio of time asleep to time in bed)
- reduced total sleep time
- reduced sleep duration and continuity
- night awakening marked by long periods of time awake.

Apparently, I've always had abnormal sleeping habits. Sometimes it takes me a long time to fall asleep. Some nights I wake up a half dozen times; others I wake up at 3:00 a.m. feeling like it's the middle of the afternoon. I can hit the ground running at 5:00 a.m. with an energy level that seems to make people angry. Recently I've started shift sleeping more often, perhaps thanks to the hormonal changes of perimenopause.

Curious about how common insomnia is in autistic people, I was shocked to learn that the prevalence of insomnia in children on the spectrum is 40 to 80 percent.[1] Yet, in reading about typical symptoms of autism and Asperger's, sleep disturbance is not only missing from the core list of diagnostic symptoms, it's rarely mentioned at all.

A BUDDING INSOMNIAC

My parents adopted a benign disinterest when it came to my sleep habits. They put me in bed at eight o'clock and the rest was up to me. I'd make multiple trips to the bathroom for a drink of water or to take one last pee (three or four or more times) but as long I didn't bother my parents, they didn't make a fuss about whether I was actually sleeping.

I had a nightlight beside my bed and most nights I'd hang over the side of the bed, reading until I felt tired. Before I was old enough to read, I would sit at the top of the steps and listen to what was going on downstairs to pass the time. In my teens I got a portable black and white TV for my birthday and I'd watch TV, using earphones so I wouldn't disturb the rest of the house.

I think my parents knew about these habits—they occasionally pointed out that I'd go blind if I kept up my "reading in the dark" and more than once they shooed me

1 Souders, M.C., Mason, T.B.A., Valladwes, O., Bucan, M. *et al.* (2009) "Sleep behaviors and sleep quality in children with autism spectrum disorders." *Sleep 32*, 12, 1566–1578.

back to bed from the bottom of the steps. On an average night, though, my parents' bedside lights had been turned off by the time I made my last couple of trips to the bathroom.

This laissez-faire attitude toward my sleep problems taught me two things: (1) it's not a big deal and (2) you're responsible for putting yourself to sleep. The second part sounds a bit harsh, but because they never made an issue out of when or how much I was sleeping, it never felt that way. A little lonely perhaps, but I also liked those few hours at night when everyone else was asleep and the house was quiet. I got to indulge in my special interest (reading) and that was calming, which eventually lulled me to sleep.

Granted, if I'd been destructive or intent on going out to roam the neighborhood, this strategy wouldn't have worked. Fortunately, we found a reasonable middle ground and I grew up with no idea that my sleep habits were abnormal.

As an adult I've learned that having the right sleep conditions makes a big difference for me. Some things that help me sleep better:

1. *Plenty of exercise during the day*. I need to be physically tired to sleep well so getting an hour of light to moderate exercise daily is essential.

2. *Heavy blankets*. The slight pressure of a heavy comforter and blankets relaxes me. Some nights, if I'm feeling very over-stimulated, I bring my weighted blanket to bed and put it on top of the comforter for extra weight. I also like to use my weighted blanket while watching TV in the evening to help my body begin to relax in preparation for bedtime.

3. *A cool room*. I tend to overheat when I sleep, so I need a cooler than average room temperature to sleep comfortably. Temperature regulation or sensitivity

to changes in body temperature are both common in autistic adults.

4. *Comfortable clothes*. As a kid I wore snug fitting pajamas. I still can't sleep in anything that's too loose, like a nightgown, because I end up feeling like it's strangling me the first time I turn over.

5. *Familiar surroundings*. It's much easier to relax when I'm in a familiar environment. If I go on vacation or move to a new place, it takes me a few days to "learn" to sleep there because my brain needs to catalog the unfamiliar sounds and smells.

6. *A quiet environment or consistent noise*. I need either total quiet or a consistent natural noise (wind, waves, steady traffic) to fall asleep. Something like intermittent voices, a radio or a television—even one playing in the apartment above me or in an adjoining hotel room—will keep me awake. In fact, I'll usually be awake long after it stops because of the anxiety it generates.

7. *A dark room*. I can't sleep unless the room is completely dark. Light shining in my room through a window or under/around a door will keep me up. The flashing light of a muted television is downright upsetting.

8. *Reading before bed*. Reading has been one of my special interests since childhood. Like any special interest, it distracts and calms me. It's also become a sleep cue. When I pick up a book in bed, my brain starts sending out sleep signals to my body. It usually only takes 15–20 minutes of reading before I start to feel myself drifting off.

9. *A light dinner and no snacks after dinner*. I fall asleep faster and sleep better if I have a low-fat, low-sugar dinner and

give myself at least a few hours to digest it before going to bed.

10. *Melatonin.* I take 5mg of melatonin about a half hour before bedtime. While melatonin doesn't work for everyone, I've found it helps me fall asleep and sleep more deeply. It hasn't cured my insomnia, but it has made it less severe.

IMPORTANT INFORMATION ABOUT MELATONIN

If you're considering taking melatonin as a sleep enhancer, there are some things you should know:

- Melatonin makes you sleepy. Take it only at bedtime.
- High doses of melatonin have been associated with increased depression and psychosis in people already suffering from these conditions. Also, women who are pregnant or trying to become pregnant, nursing mothers, and individuals with cancer, leukemia, lymphoma, multiple myeloma, or Hodgkin's disease should not take melatonin. It's a good idea to *consult with your doctor before starting the use of a melatonin supplement, especially if you are currently being treated for any other condition or taking any type of medication.*
- In the US, you can buy melatonin over the counter at stores that sell vitamins and supplements. It comes in 0.75 to 5mg doses. Taking the smallest effective dose is safer.
- Melatonin makes you feel drowsy and relaxed but not drugged, so you should still be able to easily wake if necessary, for example to respond to a family emergency.
- It's often recommended that you take melatonin every other day so you don't inhibit natural production.

- Some people take melatonin for a few weeks, then take a week off on the belief that it loses its effectiveness if taken continuously.
- If you feel groggy in the morning, try reducing the dosage.
- Other side effects can include mild headache, upset stomach, lower sex drive, and depression. Reducing the dosage can alleviate side effects. Most people don't experience any side effects at a dosage of 1mg.
- Some people experience rebound insomnia when they stop taking melatonin. One way to lessen the likelihood of rebound insomnia is to taper off, using lower dosages over one to two weeks if you decide you no longer need to take it.

I've read that autistic children often grow out of sensory sensitivities or sleep problems or clumsiness, but that hasn't been true for me or for many other autistic adults. Some of my sensitivities have lessened since childhood, but others have worsened. Perimenopause has exacerbated my sleep problems. I'm more coordinated now than I was as a child, but I'm still clumsier than the average adult.

Our autistic bodies are with us for life. Adaptations, supports, and coping strategies can lessen the negative impact on our daily lives but there isn't a lot of information available for autistic adults to help us anticipate how our bodies might change as we age.

What Does It Mean to Grow Older on the Spectrum?

I don't feel middle aged but my body tells me otherwise. My hair is going steadily gray and I've got the beginnings of arthritis in my hands. My joints pop and crack after I've been sitting too long. I'm in denial about my need for reading glasses. Pretty standard growing older stuff, whether you're on the spectrum or not.

It's the nonstandard stuff I've been wondering about over this past year.

Now that I know why I struggle with motor coordination, I wonder if I'll be able to avoid a serious fall when I'm less physically resilient. In the past month I've taken a couple of dives, one while running on a country road and one on the slippery locker room floor after swimming. The first got me a nasty case of road rash and the second resulted in a sore shoulder—relatively minor injuries considering how hard I went crashing to the ground both times. I doubt that will be the case if I take a similar fall a couple of decades from now.

I wonder if my declining mental and physical endurance will eventually limit my capacity to work or do other things I enjoy as I get older. Since hitting my 40s, I've noticed that I tire more quickly during tasks requiring intense concentration. Powering through is no longer as appealing or even as feasible as it was ten years ago. To compensate, I've been taking more breaks during the workday and giving myself permission to rest when I need to. I set smaller goals and reward myself for reaching them. I try not to have unrealistic expectations of what I can accomplish in a day.

I wonder if exercise will continue to be as valuable to me as my body ages. I need a fairly high level of activity to get the calming and regulating effects of exercise. If I can't maintain a regular exercise routine, I'll need to find alternative ways of self-regulating.

I wonder if menopause will affect me differently than it affects neurotypical women. I've noticed that there is overlap between some common traits of ASD and some symptoms of perimenopause. Many autistic women—myself included—

already struggle with the sleep problems, temperature regulation, forgetfulness, mood swings (irritability, depression, anxiety), and fatigue that are part of menopause. Will this make menopause less difficult because I have coping strategies in place that I can ramp up or will it make it more difficult by compounding my existing difficulties?

Unfortunately, information about aging on the spectrum—particularly the physical aspects of aging—is practically nonexistent. The same is true of information for coping with sensory sensitivities and satisfying sensory-seeking needs in autistic adults.

Autistic bodies don't come with a user's manual. Sometimes that's frightening.

In the course of documenting my first year of knowing I was autistic, I began to notice a worsening problem with "missing words" in my writing. The missing words are small but important, like "not," "an" and "the." I need to proofread multiple times to catch them, often in alternative formats, because my brain likes to help me out by pretending the missing word exists and skimming right over the omission.

I had dismissed the missing word problem as a quirk until it began to worsen to the point that I was missing at least one word in every few paragraphs. Then I started to get worried. Reading about aphasia—a disruption in language that can cause difficulty with finding the right word or using incorrect words as well as missing words—didn't help.

"What if my autistic brain predisposes me to aphasia?" I immediately thought.

I do sometimes use the wrong word without noticing. In writing, it tends to be a word that is close in spelling or sound, though not necessarily in meaning, like "bring" instead of "brain." When speaking, my substitutions are more entertaining. For example, recently Sang was using a kitchen towel to clean up a mess.

"Put that in the dishwasher when you're done," I suggested helpfully.

He looked at the towel and frowned. "You mean the washing machine."

Right. That's exactly what I meant. And what I thought I'd said. This happens a few times a week and I rarely notice that I've done it until someone points it out. It's more common when I'm fatigued or in a setting with a lot of distractions, which is often the case with my autistic traits.

I also have trouble with retrieving words, especially names of people and things. Here's a typical example that happened as we were straightening up the apartment one day: "I'll recycle the, the..." I was staring at the newspaper and pointing at the newspaper and I could not for the life of me come up with the word for it. All I had was a blank—a tangible, almost physical hole in my mind where "newspaper" should be. "I'll recycle that that...thing after I finish reading it. $%&*! WHY ARE THERE SO MANY DIFFERENT WORDS FOR THINGS?!"

I'd been attributing the increasing frequency of gaps in word retrieval to getting older. It's frustrating, especially when I'm trying to find the right word for a written piece and it refuses to surface. Sometimes it will be hours before I can come up with the word I'm looking for; fortunately, I've learned how to set the problem to process in the background. This often results in me randomly exclaiming words like "dichotomy!" at inappropriate times.

My language glitches have become frequent enough in the last two to three years that I can no longer ignore them. The missing words. The struggle to retrieve words. The odd, unpredictable substitutions. Sang says that my receptive language difficulties also seem to have gotten worse in the past year. I ask him to repeat himself a lot, especially when he's not facing me and I don't have the advantage of watching his lips.

Maybe the memory problems that are common to menopause are playing a role in exacerbating my already challenged language system. Maybe the natural aging process is taking a toll on my ability to compensate for my autism-related difficulties with language. Maybe it's neither.

Because there is no owner's manual for my aging autistic body, I watch and wait. I catalog and experiment and collect data. I write and read and talk with other autistic adults, comparing notes on our experiences to look for commonalities and patterns.

We are collectively writing the owner's manual for our bodies, one page at a time. I hope the generations who follow us will find them useful.

9

Exploring the Emotional Landscape

A typical Aspie–NT conversation about feelings:

NT: What's wrong?

Aspie: I don't know.

NT: You look upset.

Aspie: …

NT: Are you sad? Angry?

Aspie: I don't know.

NT: It's okay. You can tell me.

Aspie: …

NT: Fine. Don't tell me. I was just trying to help.

When an Aspie says they don't know what they're feeling, it's a literal statement. We aren't trying to dodge the conversation. We aren't withholding information. We aren't being rude, mean, cold, coy, or vindictive.

I've had variations on the above conversation many times and it's as frustrating for me as it is for the person who wants to know what's wrong. The reason? I have difficulty identifying my emotions and even more trouble verbalizing them.

Early in my first year after being diagnosed as autistic, I created emotional constellations—visual maps of how I experience happiness, sadness, and anger—to help me identify some of the specific issues I have in processing and identifying feelings.

I discovered that my difficulties fell into three general categories:

- *Modulation*: Regulating the strength of my own emotions.
- *Identification*: Identifying emotions in others.
- *Discrimination*: Separating emotion directed at me from general expressions of emotion.

MODULATION: THE BROKEN VOLUME CONTROL

There is a common misconception that autistic people are unemotional. This is often refuted by autistics themselves, who say they are *too* emotional. So which is it? For me, it's both. My emotions gravitate toward the extremes of muted or intense; few emotional experiences fall in the midranges.

My default emotional state is neutral. I don't feel especially good or bad. I'm present in the moment and content to be so. Externally, I may come across as serious or subdued, but reduced expressiveness shouldn't be confused with a negative state of being or a lack of feeling.

The feelings are definitely there. Most of the time they quietly mind their own business and I need to consciously check in to see what they're up to. When they decide to fully surface on their own, however, they're intense.

Unlike most people, I don't have a lot of ability to modulate the strength of my emotions. Imagine a radio with an on–off switch and a faulty volume control.

If you think about this in terms of weak executive function, it makes sense. Humans use reasoning, rationalization, and labeling to modulate emotion. All of these methods fall under the umbrella of executive function. Labeling emotions, in particular, seems to be hard for Aspies.

IDENTIFICATION: THE BROKEN MIRROR

Just as I have difficulty labeling my own emotions, I have trouble identifying what others are feeling. I struggle with interpreting facial expressions and body language. I'm weak at perspective-taking. Basically, when it comes to reading emotional clues, I'm like one of those old-time detectives who had to solve murders without any forensic evidence. There's only so much information you can glean from what people tell you outright.

This difficulty determining what others are feeling is a big contributor to the stereotype of the empathy-deficient Aspie. If someone is giving off "I'm sad" cues that I fail to recognize, when I don't console them they'll assume I'm cold and unsympathetic.

For neurotypical people, emotional interaction is like looking in a mirror. They expect to see a reflective emotion looking back at them and when they don't, they assume the mirror is broken.

This isn't to say I'm oblivious to other people's emotional states. I get the obvious ones and the ones that I can derive from contextual clues. What I tend to miss are subtle or unexpected emotional states.

DISCRIMINATION: MISSING THE TARGET

I've always been disturbed by confrontation and conflict, even when I'm only a bystander. By default, Sang is in charge of Confrontation With Others. If something needs to be argued over or complained about—a botched repair job or an overcooked restaurant meal—that's his department. While he's making that phone call or waiting for the manager to appear, I go off and hide.

As an adult, I'm not proud of this. Why do I desperately need to flee a situation where I'm nothing more than an observer?

Because, I've realized, I don't discriminate between anger that is aimed at me and anger in general. When someone is angry, I invariably feel like I'm the cause or the target, even when I rationally know that I'm not.

If Sang calls me when he's having a bad day, I hear how upset he is and immediately feel distressed. Not distressed as in, "I should console my husband because he's had a bad day." I feel distressed in a "this is incredibly stressful and I want it to stop" kind of way. When confronted with emotional upset, my brain immediately goes into "fix it" mode, searching for a way to make the other person feel better so I can also relieve my own distress.

Of course, a conversation with an upset spouse is upsetting to most people. But what about a conversation between two strangers that I've merely overheard? Recently, as I ate at a restaurant, the woman at the next table was telling a story about how mad she was at her sister-in-law; I felt my blood pressure rising at the tone of her words. Words that were completely irrelevant to me.

Alexithymia

It took me a long time to discover why I respond so strongly to secondhand distress. It turns out that the three areas where I have difficulty—modulation, identification, and determination—are core traits of alexithymia.

Alexithymia (literally: *having no words for emotions*) is an impairment in identifying and describing emotions. Specifically, it's characterized by:

- difficulty identifying feelings
- difficulty distinguishing between feelings and bodily sensations related to emotional arousal
- difficulty describing feelings to others.

In addition to my difficulty with identifying and describing feelings, I'm also more likely to have physical complaints when I'm emotionally upset. I'll be feeling frustrated or sad, but complain that I'm uncomfortably cold or intolerably sleepy.

WHEN A PARTNER HAS ALEXITHYMIA

Alexithymia can have serious consequences in relationships, particularly in partner relationships. If you're alexithymic, sharing some of these suggestions with your partner may help both of you better cope with your alexithymic traits.

1. *Asking an alexithymic person how they feel can be a significant source of stress.* When you are alexithymic, figuring out how you feel about something is hard work and not always possible. It's also very easy to feel "defective" if you can't answer a seemingly simple question like, "How do you feel?"
2. *If an alexithymic person says they don't know how they feel, take it at face value.* They're not playing head games or being coy. They either don't know how they feel or don't know how to describe what they're feeling. For an alexithymic person, being asked, "How do you feel?" is the emotional equivalent of being asked, "Quick, what's 2345 x 8473?"
3. *Sometimes people experience events in ways that don't revolve around feelings.* While one person might be emotionally moved by something, another person may have been focused more on the practical, sociological, anthropological, historical, religious, mathematical, artistic,

technical, or mechanical aspect of the experience. No one way of experiencing an event is superior to another.

4. *Shaming someone for not being able to articulate how they feel does more harm than good.* Alexithymia is not an inability to show compassion or sympathy. Saying, "Use your words" or berating someone with epithets like "cold," "heartless," "selfish," or "unfeeling" only makes things worse.

5. *Sometimes an alexithymic person needs to suspend an emotionally charged conversation and revisit it later, after having time to think about how they feel.* Having a delayed emotional reaction or needing time to identify feelings is common in alexithymic people. It may take hours or days to understand what took place during an especially emotional experience.

6. *An alexithymic person will not always be able to read or respond to your emotions in the way you expect.* Alexithymia can be expressive (difficulty with our own emotions), receptive (difficulty with the emotions of others), or both. This might mean that someone is not very good at comforting a loved one, that they have trouble being around a loved one who is expressing strong emotions, or that they don't recognize what emotion a loved one is experiencing.

7. *Alexithymia does not mean that a person has no emotions.* Alexithymia is difficulty with identifying and talking about the emotions that a person does have. Sometimes those emotions are hard to identify because they're muted or jumbled up. Sometimes they're hard to identify because they're overwhelmingly intense.

8. *Alexithymia is a real impairment.* It's not the result of not trying hard enough, not paying attention to people, or being self-absorbed.

There is a high rate of alexithymia in autistic people. Not only are autistic people very likely to exhibit the characteristics of alexithymia, their parents are as well. However, many nonautistic people also have alexithymia, so it isn't exclusive to ASD.

Alexithymia isn't a clinical diagnosis like autism. It's a construct (theory) used to describe the traits of people who have difficulty verbalizing emotions. It's also a helpful way of thinking about some of the challenges that Aspies have with processing feelings.

Sketching My Emotional Constellations

HAPPINESS

Learning about the technical side of emotional dysfunction was helpful, but it felt like only half of the answer I was looking for. What I really needed to do was get in touch with my feelings. The problem was, my feelings have never been very cooperative when it comes to being named.

When I think about "happy" all I have is a blurry splotch of a feeling. "Elated," on the other hand, has a very specific shape for me—elated is riding my bike down a hill at top speed, the wind whipping my shirt, the road a blur beneath me, and I can feel a shout building in my chest that makes me want to throw my head back and close my eyes and let out a crazy loud laughing shouting whoop of joy.

As I explored happiness in more detail, sketching out a constellation of happiness-related words on paper, I was struck by how much of my emotional landscape I describe in physical terms.

"Contentment," the place where I spend the most time emotionally, is curling up on the couch with a good book, holding hands with my husband on our evening walk, watching a hawk circle overhead, sliding between freshly washed flannel sheets, seeing the sun rise on a fall morning, digging my toes into the sand at the beach, pulling on my favorite t-shirt.

One level up from contentment is "peace," the place where I most like to be. When I'm in a peaceful place, I feel a deep sense of quiet in my mind and body. Everything about the world feels right—in sync, wide open, infinite. That peacefulness almost always fills me when I'm outdoors—hiking, running, swimming, walking the dog—away from people, soaking up sunshine, covering distance, moving.

"Wonder" is a silent feeling, a sense of being awestruck. It's always unexpected and strong. Pure, childlike, fleeting. It's seeing the sun hitting an ice-coated world after a winter storm. It's driving around the bend of a mountain and having the landscape suddenly open onto a lush green caldera. It's emerging from the woods to discover a herd of elk grazing in a meadow.

The road to "bliss" runs through desserts made of chocolate, good sex or a long run on a beautiful day. Bliss defies capture. It's boneless, languid, unbound.

"Elation" is joy^2. It's that whooping, running rush of feeling, more physical than simple joy but less physical than the feeling without a name that I drew as a question mark when I made my constellation. If elation is joy squared then the unnamable feeling is joy^{1000}. It's an entirely physical sensation. It makes me want to bounce up and down, skip down the street, twirl in circles. I think this is a uniquely autistic feeling and maybe that's why I can't find an appropriate name for it. If it were possible to distill happiness down to its purest, most potent form, it would be this unnameable thing that occasionally takes over my body and makes me feel like I'm flying.

After making my happiness constellation, it became obvious to me that I associate specific physical sensations and events with emotions. For the stronger emotions, the physical sensations can verge on overwhelming. Extremely positive emotions demand to be released through some sort of physical activity, while the calmer, positive emotions bring a sense of internal quiet and physical stillness.

ANGER

I was so excited about the discoveries I'd made in creating my happiness constellation that I set out to tackle another familiar emotion: anger. While autistic people are often stereotyped as having uncontrollable bouts of anger or being angry in general, when I sat down to make my anger constellation, I only got as far as rage and frustration before I was stumped. Anger has been a familiar companion over the years, but it's one that I've relegated to the shadows.

My anger constellation turned into a chaotic, fractured, and sometimes incoherent mess—an accurate reflection of the way I experience anger itself. Anger makes me uncomfortable. I avoid it. I suppress it. Most often my reaction to any form of anger is that I want it to stop. Perhaps because I didn't learn how to express anger constructively as a child, only that it was undesirable. My literal Aspie brain didn't perceive the difference between "expressing anger *in destructive ways* is bad" and "*expressing anger* is bad." What I really needed was for someone to specifically say, "When you're mad, here are some things you can do about it."

When I look at my anger constellation, I see a few specific forms of anger that I associate with the realities of being autistic:

- *Frustration*, often the result of unmet expectations, which makes me grit my teeth and growl when what I should be doing is identifying my needs and articulating or acting on them. Serial frustration sometimes leads to a shutdown or a meltdown.

- *Annoyance* is a disruption of my process or state of mind. I can't find the right word to finish a sentence and lose the flow of what I'm writing. The people in the hotel room next to mine are watching TV when I'm trying to fall asleep. Annoyance is the fly buzzing around my head; frustration is taking 20 whacks at it and missing every time.

- *Irritability*, which has roots in sensory overload. I'm overtired. I'm hungry. I'm hot. My shirt is scratchy. I've ignored my sensory limit and it's turning me into a cranky toddler. Danger, danger, shutdown is imminent.

All three of these are a direct result of how I experience the world—of sensory sensitivities, rigid thinking, poor executive function. My first instinct when I experience them is to shut them down. It's bad enough that I'm having to deal with the triggering event, but now I have to deal with my own emotional upset on top of it and that feels like a double failure. This is some high-level, self-destructive thinking.

It's also not where my real problems with anger lie. The deeper I dug into what anger means, the darker the road ahead became. Finally, I came upon the big three: indignation, alienation, and rage. A lifetime of not understanding myself and feeling at odds with the world around me had left me with some firmly entrenched and very hard-to-face emotional skeletons in my closet.

I began with the one that's been with me the longest: indignation. *Indignation* arises from humiliation, shame, fear of not being good enough, from feeling invisible, stupid, or ignored. It's the way my vision blurs when someone treats me like I'm an idiot for asking the same question too many times. It's the hot blush I can't control when I say something that falls on deaf ears. It's the blood pounding in my head when someone lectures me like I'm a child.

Indignation is wanting to scream that I get it, I know, I understand, I'm here, I have something to say, slow down, I can do this, stop trying to fix/help/correct/educate me. It's been with me for as long as I can remember, festering in the broad gap between intellectual ability and social skill.

Alienation arrived later, sometime in early adulthood, but it sits stubbornly beside indignation with no plans to leave any time soon. It may be odd to describe alienation as an expression of anger, but as Sang put it, "You'll shut someone out for five years instead of yelling at them for five minutes." That's an exaggeration, but not by much.

My capacity for resentment is deep and wide. I lack confrontation skills. It's easier to stay mad. In my 20s and 30s, my anger fueled my actions and propelled me through a lot of pain. It's probably responsible for a good deal of my success. But clinging to that anger also cut me off from people in deep, possibly irreparable, ways.

Finally, there were the nightmares filled with *rage*. When I first started having these nightmares about ten years ago, the intensity of them was startling. I would wake up thinking, "Who is that crazy woman?" For a while, I thought there was something seriously wrong with me. I've since concluded that those particular nightmares were a form of meltdown. After getting my official diagnosis, they stopped.

What hasn't stopped is the kind of anger that goes straight to my hands. In the same way that I experience pure undistilled happiness, I also experience a very pure form of anger. It starts in my brain and terminates in my hands. It's reflexive. White hot. Short-lived. Irrational. More chemical or electrical than emotional.

Occasionally, if I'm on the edge of that kind of anger and Sang bumps into me in the kitchen, I irrationally, impulsively get the urge to punch him. I'm not mad at him. I'm not mad at all, in the typical sense. I'm experiencing the emotional equivalent of touching my hand to a hot stove. Trigger → physical impulse to react. There's no cognitive processing involved. I'm not thinking. I'm reacting.

This feeling is almost always triggered by a physical experience and only happens when I'm hovering near my limit for sensory stimulation. I've learned to control the physical impulse. The trigger hits, I feel a spike of intense negative energy surge from my head down my spine, and I still my hands until it passes.

That last part is key. If I didn't hold on tight and ride out the physical impulse, I would lash out with my hands at whatever was nearby, punching, throwing, or breaking something to dissipate the energy in my hands.

SADNESS

I saved my sadness constellation for last. Sadness feels like the emotion that is most strongly connected to humanity—the one that binds us to each other in some important and primitive way. I can be happy by myself. I'm as likely to be angry with myself as with someone else. But sadness—I usually need another person to tip me over into feeling sad.

Like my anger constellation, making my sadness constellation required a thesaurus. Once I got past grief, depression, and resignation, I needed help identifying other types of sad feelings. But unlike my exploration of anger, the thesaurus wasn't much help this time. I added a few more words to the constellation, but I'm not sure how strongly I experience any of them.

Sadness feels like a diffuse emotion, more of a background state of being than a tangible feeling. I'm rarely actively sad. I don't burst into tears when I hear sad news. The last time I cried at a movie, I was 12. The only book that ever made me tear up was *A Prayer for Owen Meany*. More than once

I've sat stoically immobile beside someone I love while they broke down.

My sadness is all undercurrent, twisted up inside me, unable to escape to the surface. This, of course, makes me look cold and unfeeling. The stereotypical emotionless Aspie.

The first time I confronted my muted sadness was in high school. A girl in my class, Karen, was killed in a car accident. The entire junior class attended her funeral, and everyone sobbed from beginning to end. Except me.

I remember standing there, my best friend crying against my shoulder, and feeling…confused. I barely knew Karen. She was one of the "fast" girls, part of a small clique that didn't mix in with the rest of the class much. Many of the girls crying that day in church wouldn't have hesitated to whisper something mean about Karen or her friends when she was alive. Yet here they were, brokenhearted. It made no sense to me.

Of course I felt sad that she'd died. It was a horrible tragedy. But obviously I didn't feel as sad as everyone else. If I had, wouldn't I be crying too? Soon this thought consumed me. In desperation, I tried to make myself cry by thinking of sad things, by focusing on how tragic the day was. I squeezed my eyes tightly closed until they started to water. A few teardrops fell but mostly what I felt was a sick, sinking panic.

While everyone was mourning the loss of our classmate, I alone was wondering: "What's wrong with me?" And afterwards, while everyone was getting drunk to soothe their pain, I was hoping that if I got drunk enough, I'd somehow gain access to this mysterious thing called grief.

While I've experienced loss since then, my experience of "grief" is still uneven and unpredictable. Sometimes my reaction to death is a sadness so strong and overpowering that it becomes physically painful. Other times I feel like my grief is strangled inside me with only the smallest of escape valves to trickle through. In this sense, grief frightens me. I worry that I haven't practiced enough and when the big day comes, I'll be unprepared, like a boxer entering a title match with only a few amateur bouts under her belt.

Asperger's is such a paradoxical condition. I love being alone but I fear abandonment. I don't often experience unmitigated grief but when I do, it's overwhelming. I need a thesaurus to help me identify the shape of my feelings, but once I put names to them, they come alive for me in vividly specific ways.

Since learning more about ASD and alexithymia I've come to wonder if my muted experience of sadness is a self-protective mechanism. When I wrote about happiness and anger, I talked about the unfiltered versions of these emotions that I experience—the emotions that feel particularly autistic in nature.

I'm far less equipped to handle unfiltered sadness. When it comes, it's crushing. I think my subconscious instinct is to mute the intensity. There is, after all, only so much sadness a person can handle. So I experience sadness in my own way, inwardly, quietly.

There is a theory that sadness serves an important purpose in our lives: triggering reflection after a major life event. When we experience loss or a setback, it makes sense for us to withdraw inward and reevaluate our lives. The result is often a life-changing insight or decision.

In this sense, my sadness serves me well. I turn inward, often and intensely, searching for answers, insight, a truer path. Even at that funeral in high school, in the absence of grief, I was looking inward, sad in my own way. Sad, perhaps, in a very similar way to the rest of the girls, though I didn't understand it then.

As an adult, I know that the teenage girls in that church were mourning more than the loss of a classmate. They were mourning the loss of their own innocence. They were confronting the cruelty of life. They were facing the dangers that adulthood holds, the possibility that it could have been any one of us rocketing down the highway one moment, dead at the bottom of a cliff the next.

They were sad for Karen, sad for themselves, frightened, overwhelmed. When I look at it in that context, I see that my feelings weren't that different from theirs. However, back then, I didn't understand why they were so sad. I was struggling with something autistic people often struggle with: perspective taking.

At the time, this was probably mistaken by my classmates for a lack of empathy.

The Empathy Conundrum

It's true, I lack empathy.

By lack, I don't mean a complete absence of empathy. It's more accurate to say that I have an empathy deficiency. If most adults are doing empathy at the calculus level, I'm still in Algebra II and solving for X in ways that would make most people's heads spin.

From my initial reading about ASD, I assumed that my impaired empathy was typical for someone with Asperger's. Much of the published literature includes impaired empathy as a common ASD trait. "Lack of social or emotional reciprocity" is one of the diagnostic criteria. My own experience didn't disprove that.

Then I discovered the online autism community and suddenly felt like I needed to hide my struggles with empathy. Everywhere I looked autistics and allies were refuting the notion that autistics lack empathy. Again and again I encountered discussions about empathy online and quietly slunk away, feeling like there was something wrong with me—like I was a "defective" autistic.

I Googled empathy—probably one too many times. I read the long list of definitions at Wikipedia. I read Simon Baron-Cohen's writing on the subject. I read looooong threads on Wrong Planet and Facebook. I revisited the diagnostic criteria. I combed through the #actuallyautistic tag, reading firsthand accounts by autistic people on Tumblr.

The more I read, the more confused I became. I started to wonder if I was talking about the same thing others were talking about when I use the word empathy.

What is empathy, exactly? What are we talking about when we talk about empathy?

SYMPATHY VS. EMPATHY

Empathy, in the most basic sense, is the ability to understand and share an emotional state with another person.

As an adult with a good amount of life experience, I can often understand the emotional state of another person. I know that if someone's dog has died, they'll feel sad. Most people probably come to this conclusion in a more instinctive way than I do, but I get there all the same.

Depending on the situation, I may share an emotional state with another person to some degree. I know how I felt when my dog died. Logically I know that the other person feels very sad. If I knew the person's dog, I'll feel a sense of loss myself, and that will contribute to my sharing their emotional state. However, I rarely experience a strong emotional reaction to another person's circumstances.

That's not to say that I don't experience concern toward other people. Simple concern for others, though, isn't so much empathy as sympathy. Sympathy is a concern for the wellbeing of another person. It can exist in the absence of the empathic act of sharing an emotional state with that person. It often arises from empathy, but it doesn't have to.

When my daughter says she's had a bad day at work, even though I find it hard to share her emotional state, I sympathize with her frustration or sadness. I don't know what it feels like to get a phone call from a suddenly homeless student. I can't truly share what my daughter is feeling as she tells me about the experience. But I do worry about her ability to cope with the situation. I understand how important her work is to her. I hear the distress in her voice and want to do what I can to offer comfort.

In this type of situation, I have a great deal of sympathy, regardless of how strongly rooted in empathy my concern is. My sympathy doesn't always come across like a neurotypical person's sympathy would— it rarely does—but it exists just the same.

THE CHALLENGES OF PERSPECTIVE TAKING

The examples I used above are fairly explicit in terms of the emotional content of the situation. Both a dead dog or a student who's been kicked out of her home have obvious contextual clues to the emotions that are present. Even my rudimentary empathic radar is going to pick them up.

Where I struggle most is in subtle situations. I often say things that other people consider insensitive and then I completely miss their wounded reaction to my comment. Why? Because I didn't know that my comment was insensitive in the first place and I have trouble reading nonverbal communication.

Imagine that your friend's dog has died but you don't know that yet. When you speak to them, you'd pick up that something was wrong, but it would be hard to truly comprehend how they feel until they explain the source of their distress.

For me, all the little things that people communicate nonverbally or hint at or imply are like a whole bunch of secretly dead dogs. Until some says, "Your comment hurt my feelings because…" all I have is a vague feeling that something is off. Maybe not even that.

This is why I "failed" the Sally–Anne test. Twice. I failed it when I first discovered it early in my reading about Asperger's and then I failed it again months later, because it was presented in a slightly different format.

If you've never seen the Sally–Anne test, it's a simple playacted scene in which the Sally puppet puts a marble in a basket. She then leaves the room and the Anne puppet moves the marble to another basket. The viewer is then asked to predict where Sally will look for the marble when she returns to the room. Autistic children will often say that Sally should look in the second basket because they don't recognize that Sally was out of the room when Anne moved the marble. They assume that Sally has the same information that they, the viewer, have.

It's easy argue that the Sally–Anne test has little to do with empathy, and that's true, the test doesn't predict the emotional dimension of empathy. Taking the test doesn't require you to share an emotional state with Sally. It does, however, require you to set aside your own knowledge of the situation and take Sally's perspective.

This is where a more precise definition of empathy comes in handy. Empathy has two components: cognitive (perspective taking) and affective (emotional response to another's emotional state). The Sally–Anne test is a test of cognitive empathy, which is impaired in people on the spectrum.

This is why I can fail a simple test twice, even when I already know the correct answer. I automatically default to my own perspective. I can take another person's perspective, but it often requires a conscious decision on my part to do so. When I say I have an empathy deficiency, I mean that I rarely take the view of another person spontaneously and instinctively. I lack cognitive empathy.

However, when it comes to affective empathy, according to a 2007 study,[1] Aspies are on a par with neurotypicals. In fact, autistic people are often described as having too much empathy. While I think the people using this phrase mean well, I'm not sure it's accurate. Is the autistic person who feels overwhelmed by an emotional situation truly *sharing and understanding the emotional state of another person too much* or are they overwhelmed by an inability to regulate their own reaction to a highly charged situation? These are two different conditions, though they may look the same externally.

When I feel overwhelmed by another person's emotions, it's related to my difficulty regulating my own emotions and my struggle with discriminating between emotions that are aimed at me and emotions that are aimed at someone else. If I encounter two people having a shouting argument, my emotional reaction is the same as if I were the target of their shouting, as if they were both angry *at me*.

I feel frightened and intimidated. I feel an intense need to escape from a situation to which I'm nothing more than a bystander. Notice that I don't feel anything empathically in relation to the other two people. The only person I'm thinking about is myself and how uncomfortable I am. My distress at the situation might outwardly appear to be empathic but my internal reaction is a great big "MAKE IT STOP, NOW."

In the 2007 study mentioned above, researchers found similar reactions in Aspie participants who scored significantly higher on a scale of personal distress than neurotypical participants, indicating "a greater tendency to have

1 Rogers, K., Dziobek, I. *et al.* (2007) "Who cares? Revisiting empathy in Asperger Syndrome." *Journal of Autism and Developmental Disorders 37*, 709–715.

self-oriented feelings of anxiety and discomfort in response to tense interpersonal settings."

WHAT DOES A LACK OF EMPATHY MEAN?

Empathy has many definitions, but they all have at their core understanding the emotional state of another person. When I say I lack empathy, what I mean is I have a deficit in understanding the emotional states of others, just like I have a deficit in understanding my own emotional states.

This doesn't mean I'm unsympathetic or that I don't care for others. It doesn't mean I have no emotions.

It does mean I may need more information than a typical person to understand a social situation. That my reactions to other people's emotions may be unconventional. That I have to work harder to grasp what comes naturally to most people.

It also means that I've been called cold, selfish, and mean when what I was feeling was overwhelmed, confused, or frightened. The dual challenges of impaired perspective taking and impaired emotional awareness have made emotional connection one of the most difficult aspects of relating to others.

10

Executive Function

The Brain's Control Center

When I was in middle school, I spent a week visiting my college-age cousin in Brooklyn. It all felt very grown-up, with her living in the studio apartment she shared with a roommate and me on my first extended trip away from home.

She was my favorite cousin—someone I thought was smart and cool and funny—and I assumed she'd have all sorts of exciting things planned for us. Once I got settled in, she asked me, "What do you want to do?"

"I don't know." I had no idea. The city seemed impossibly big and, being from the suburbs of Connecticut, I couldn't imagine what city people did.

She seemed frustrated by my answer and that made me a little annoyed. She lived here. Shouldn't she have a plan? What kind of person invites someone for a week-long visit with no plan?

"What kinds of things are there to do?" I asked.

She looked at me like, "What kind of person doesn't know what there is to do in New York?"

Clearly, we were at an impasse. We went for a walk around her neighborhood, then we went to paint a room in the brownstone owned by her boyfriend's medical school professor. The professor was on vacation, so we got to cook out in his miniature garden after we'd finished painting.

Throughout the day, the "What do you want to do?" conversation came up a few more times, and each time I could tell she was growing more exasperated, while I grew more panicked.

I had no idea what I wanted to do; she—and now her boyfriend and roommate—couldn't believe this was possible.

I couldn't even come up with the simplest suggestion like, "I want a cheeseburger" or "I want to see the Empire State Building." Every time she asked what I wanted to do, my mind went completely blank and then flooded with panicked variations of "What's wrong with me?"

Finally, as we were finishing up dinner at the professor's brownstone, my cousin handed me the current edition of *The New Yorker*. "Here," she said, "look through the events in the front and find something you want to do this week."

"Like what?" I asked, still not getting it.

"Anything," she replied.

I flipped through the pages, reading the listings for movies and art shows. Choosing still seemed impossible, even now that I had a finite list to pick from. Comparing each option with all the others was overwhelming, and what if I picked the wrong thing and they thought I was weird? I'd learned by then that I had weird interests for my age and gender.

I eventually put the magazine down and the three of them looked at me expectantly. "What do you guys want to do?" I asked.

"Do you like comedy?" my cousin's roommate asked, perhaps out of desperation.

"Yes!" Yes, I did. I loved sitcoms and stand-up comics. In fact, before my cousin moved away, we used to enjoy listening to her Steve Martin albums together.

"Why didn't you say so?" the roommate asked.

Because even though I like comedy and it was a favorite way to spend time with my cousin, it just didn't occur to me.

For an Aspie, this is a familiar occurrence. It happens when someone asks me what I want to eat or what my favorite color is or where I want to go on vacation. In my head, these questions have an infinite number of possible answers and I don't know how to begin narrowing the possibilities down.

Even the simplest decisions can tie me up in knots. In part, this is because my poor natural decision-making skills have led me to develop some less-than-helpful workarounds when it comes to decision making, including:

- *What do* you *want*? I've noticed that other people often have stronger preferences or are more aware of what they want or like than I am. If what they suggest isn't objectionable to me, I'll go along with their choice because it's easy.

- *I don't want A, so by default I must want B.* If someone says, "Do you want Chinese food or pizza?" it rarely occurs to me that I actually want a burger.

- *This is too hard. I give up.* When there are too many options, I have trouble figuring out where to start. I end up choosing the first option that isn't terrible. These are usually the choices I end up feeling most ambivalent about.

- *I want A but it's too much work so I'll settle for B.* This tends to be the result of making decisions when I'm overloaded. I would love ice cream right now but going out to get it sounds exhausting so I'll have this peach instead.

- *I want this thing and nothing else.* This sounds great. It's not. What I want is often imaginary. In my head it's this perfect thing. In reality, it's often a pale shadow of what I anticipated.

- *I want A, but I can tell you want B. If one of us has to be disappointed, I'd rather it be me.* This makes me sound like a martyr. Honestly, it's an annoying reflex response that I need to cure myself of because done too often, it breeds resentment.

My difficulties with narrowing down options from an amorphous, infinite number of choices to one concrete thing affects more than my decision-making abilities. If someone hands me a piece of paper and says, "Draw something," my immediate reaction is, "But what?"

I never open up my word processing software unless I have a firm idea of what I want to write. To open a blank document with no idea of where I plan to start writing is unthinkable. It would be completely unproductive. I'd be better off taking a nap because at least then I wouldn't be beating myself up over how bad I am at spontaneously coming up with creative ideas.

"Just think" is a common phrase of encouragement when someone draws a blank. But for Aspies, the harder we try, the more elusive the answer becomes. The biggest problem is that when I "just think" in those situations, I'm devoting 90 percent of my thoughts and energy to the fact that I can't think of an answer and how stupid that must be making me look.

When All You Can Draw Is a Blank

Decision making and planning—the things that I struggled with during that week in New York and still struggle with today—are aspects of executive function (EF), which is a fancy term for our ability to monitor and control our actions. Other cognitive functions that fall under the executive function umbrella include working memory, paying attention, mental flexibility, error detection and correction, applying past knowledge to present situations, behavior inhibition, and starting, stopping, or changing tasks.

It can be hard to identify areas of your life where your EF is impaired because the definition of the elements that make up EF is so broad. Difficulty switching between tasks could mean any of these things:

- *Difficulty stopping one thing and starting another*—for example, difficulty with stopping a favorite activity on the computer and starting on cleaning your room.

- *Difficulty shifting attention from one thing to another because you're so engaged in the first task/subject*—for example, you're watching TV and you hear someone in the room speaking to you, but the content of what they're saying doesn't register and you have no idea what they said.

- *Difficulty with flexible thinking*—for example, you're trying to fix something and can't see that doing it another way would be faster or more effective.

- *Difficulty returning to doing something when interrupted.*

Each subcategory of executive function has many, many applications in daily life. Consider how many decisions you make in a day or even in an hour. Everything from what to eat and what to wear to how to spend your Saturday afternoon and whether you'll need a coat for the walk to the bus. Once you make the decision, you have to plan how to carry it out, execute it, correct any errors you make...all tasks that call on executive function capabilities.

AN EXECUTIVE FUNCTION PRIMER

Executive function is a broad term that refers to the cognitive processes that help us regulate, control, and manage our thoughts and actions. It includes planning, working memory, attention, problem solving, verbal reasoning, inhibition, cognitive flexibility, initiation of actions, and monitoring of actions.

That's a nice textbook definition, but what does executive function look like in real life? Sometimes it looks like responsibility. Sometimes it looks like self-discipline. Sometimes it looks like being a competent adult. Most people on the spectrum have some level of executive function impairment, but how that impairment impacts our lives can vary greatly from person to person. Thinking about each of the executive function processes individually can help us identify the areas that we struggle most with, which can make finding solutions easier.

Planning

Planning is a series of subtasks that, ideally, leads to the accomplishment of a goal. The planning process includes assessing needs, formulating options, evaluating those options, and sequencing the selected options to achieve a goal. People who have difficulties with planning are often disorganized or struggle to complete complex tasks that have many steps. But they may also have a hard time with things like driving, cooking, household chores, shopping, or even walking across an unfamiliar room without bumping into furniture—all common tasks that require the sort of planning many people take for granted.

Problem Solving

Problem solving is a process of identifying and overcoming obstacles to reach a predefined goal. Probably the most complex cognitive process that we engage in, it draws on all of the other aspects of executive function. The traditional problem-solving process includes identifying and defining the problem, forming a strategy, organizing information, allocating resources, monitoring your progress, and evaluating the results. If just reading that sentence was overwhelming, you're not alone. Difficulties with problem solving can cause people to "freeze up" when faced with an unexpected obstacle or to completely miss the fact that a problem exists. It may look like we're avoiding a problem, when in fact we have no idea where to begin solving it.

Verbal Reasoning

Verbal reasoning is the ability to understand, analyze and think critically about concepts presented in words. Often verbal reasoning also has a social component. To successfully analyze another person's words, we need to understand the coded social messages that underpin those words. Verbal reasoning can also rely on the ability to think in gray areas or to make temporary but illogical assumptions, which is often counterintuitive for people on the spectrum. Difficulties with verbal reasoning make it hard to accurately take notes on a lecture, answer reading comprehension questions, retell stories, solve math word problems, or follow spoken instructions.

Working Memory

We use our working memory to hold pieces of information in our mind for a short amount of time while completing a task. Common examples are remembering a phone number while dialing it or remembering a set of names while searching for them in a list. Poor working memory capacity can make a person look "spacey" or absentminded. It also makes it difficult to complete tasks that have multiple steps, especially when those steps are presented verbally.

Attention

Our brains have two competing attention systems. Executive function controls the "top down" system, purposely directing our attention to important activities. Our senses, on the other hand, control the "bottom up" system, drawing our attention to things in our environment. Because autistic individuals have so much difficulty filtering out sensory input, the bottom up system tends to dominate. That makes it harder for the top down system to intentionally "pay attention" to something. Difficulties with attention can make it hard to concentrate, especially on activities that aren't intrinsically interesting. People who struggle with attention may also find it hard to finish what they start, focus on one thing a time, stick to a schedule, be on time for activities or block out environmental distractions.

Inhibition

Inhibition is the ability to block or suppress a thought or action, either consciously or subconsciously. Our brains are constantly inhibiting—or failing to inhibit—thoughts and actions. To focus on one thing, we have to inhibit countless other distracting inputs. To remember a piece of information, we have to inhibit the retrieval of millions of irrelevant bits of information. Poor inhibition can affect everything from word retrieval while speaking to the ability to sit still while working. It's also responsible for our tendency to give long monologues in conversation or to blurt out a thought, only to regret it seconds later.

Initiation of Actions

Initiation is the "getting started" phase of an activity. It can refer to everything from starting a major project to taking a shower or preparing for bedtime. Difficulties with initiation can have a serious negative impact on self-care, a seemingly routine series of tasks that need to be initiated over and over, on a daily basis. People who have poor initiation are often labeled lazy or unmotivated. They may struggle with staying organized, keeping their living area clean, beginning important projects, or initiating major life activities like applying for a job or college.

Monitoring of Actions

This is sometimes called the troubleshooting aspect of executive function. Most of the time, monitoring takes place as a background activity. We only become conscious that we're doing it when something goes wrong and we need to make a correction. The exception is when we're doing something unfamiliar, like learning a new task, where we have to actively monitor our actions closely to quickly correct errors. Often, impaired monitoring means that even familiar tasks require active monitoring, slowing down our performance, making it hard to multitask, or making us feel self-conscious about an activity. People who struggle with monitoring may find it hard to learn new tasks quickly, perform familiar activities under stress, spot mistakes in their work, or complete a familiar task in an unfamiliar environment.

Cognitive Flexibility

Cognitive flexibility is the ability to shift your thinking or attention in response to a change in the environment or situation (new rules, information, demands, or goals). It also refers to the ability to switch between tasks as well as the ability to consider multiple aspects of a situation at once, such as seeing opposing points of view. Impaired cognitive flexibility results in resistance to change, rigid thinking, a strong reliance on routines, and difficulty seeing a situation from another person's point of view.

Poor executive function is why an autistic person can ace IQ tests but not be able to complete a project, get to class on time, prepare a meal, or do any number of seemingly simple things that require being organized, completing many tasks in sequence, or planning ahead.

Frustratingly, an executive function deficit is not something you can fix by simply trying harder. Often, other people will look at the symptoms of impaired executive function and assume the autistic person is lazy, spaced out, or disorganized. If only they would make more effort, everything could be fixed. In fact, I think most autistic people—including me—think this of themselves at times.

On top of this, executive functioning capacity can vary over time. You may find that there are days when you are much more functional and days when even the simplest tasks require an exhausting amount of effort. Executive function impairments may worsen during times of stress or fatigue. In the longer term, many people notice that their EF took a downturn during adolescence or early adulthood. Some women also find that perimenopause is another time when EF impairments become more significant.

While you can't fix an EF deficit, you can learn ways to compensate. Visual schedules, reminders, to-do lists, incentives, stim toys, and other accommodations can help mitigate the effects of dysfunction of the executive system on our daily lives. So can simple social scripts that buy some extra thinking time or narrow down a list of possible options. For example, if I'm visiting someone's house and they ask me what I want to drink, asking "What do you have?" makes formulating a response much easier.

A similar formula works with the wide open and commonly asked question, "What do you want to do?" A reflective reply like, "What are you in the mood for?" or "What's fun to do on a Saturday night around here?" will not only make your friend or relative feel like you care about their preferences, but will also help you shorten the list of possibilities, which can take away those long terrifying moments of your brain chanting, "I don't know" over and over.

You Can Do Something About That

Social scripts are relatively simple solutions to relatively simple executive function problems. Impaired executive function can cause more serious problems as well—problems that can be hard to identify, let alone solve, because of the way our bodies work.

In my early reading about Asperger's, I came across this idea: if something is bothering you, you can do something about it. That seems like deceptively simple advice. If you're cold, put on a sweater. If you're hungry, eat something. If the sun is in your eyes, move or close the blinds or put on your sunglasses.

For a typical person, the idea that you can get up and put on a sweater if you're cold is probably not an earth-shattering revelation. In fact, it's something they've been instinctively doing since childhood. The typical brain receives an incoming message about physical discomfort, finds a solution, and swiftly acts on it:

Typical body: I'm cold.

Typical brain: We're underdressed. Stop what we're doing and put on a sweater.

Typical body: Good idea!

This is where the typical person gets up from the computer, goes to the closet and takes out a sweater. But for a lot Aspies, the body–brain communication is dulled to the point that we appear not to feel pain, cold, or other physical sensations in the same way that typical people do. You often hear parents of autistic youngsters say that their children will play outside in the winter without wearing a coat or will injure themselves but continue playing like they haven't noticed.

Based on my experience, I don't think we necessarily *feel* pain or cold less. I think our body–brain communication is muted. As a result it takes a lot more sensory input from our bodies to provoke a reaction in our brains.

Here's how my brain functions:

Body: Something's not right.

Brain: Uh-huh...

Body: No really. I feel strange.

Brain: Yeah yeah…

Body: I think I'm cold.

Brain: Shhh, I'm busy.

Body: Yep, definitely cold.

Brain: Okay, I get it, you're cold. Hmmm…maybe we should do something about it.

Body: Look, I have goose bumps.

Brain: I'm thinking!

Body: Now I'm shivering.

Brain: Okay, go get a sweater.

Often I find myself feeling physically uncomfortable but I'm so deeply engaged in what I'm doing that the discomfort hovers at the edges of my consciousness. It exists as low-level background noise, not serious enough to make me stop and think about it, but not minor enough to completely ignore. As a result, I put up with it until it becomes truly impossible to ignore. By that point, of course, it's long past the time when I should have acted and the minor annoyance has ballooned into serious discomfort.

Even when I get to this point, I may put off stopping what I'm doing to get that sweater. Clearly there are elements of impaired executive function here. I have difficulty paying attention to changes in my environment that may necessitate planning or problem solving. I also struggle with stopping and switching tasks to attend to my needs once I identify them and formulate a plan. But the more I read about ASD, the more I started to think there was something else at work.

HOW SENSORY HYPOSENSITIVITY CAN COMPOUND EF DYSFUNCTION

Our bodies are equipped with a kind of virtual dashboard that monitors the physical sensations that originate within us. Are we low on fuel? Running too hot? Has it been too long since some critical service was performed? Is a warning light flashing? Collectively, our sensitivity to pain, temperature, itch, sensual touch, sensations from our organs and muscles, hunger, thirst, and breathlessness is called interoception.

Interoceptive feedback is important for keeping our bodies in good working condition by providing the information necessary for troubleshooting and correcting imbalances in the body. Emotions often arise from our interoceptive sensations too. When someone asks how you feel, you probably subconsciously check in with your body, and realizing that you're tired, hungry, hot, or achy, you reply, "Not too great." Conversely, if your interoceptive sensations are in balance, you might report feeling happy or at least content.

But what if your interoceptive system is dampened? What if a sensation needs to be in the red zone before it comes up on the dashboard? Well, then you forget to eat or stare in wonder at your bleeding toes or don't realize you might be in pain until you pass out. Sound familiar?

Many autistic people have dampened or muted interoception. We don't seem to notice what's going on in our bodies until it reaches a level that other people would find intolerable. And often when we do notice it, it goes from, "Oh, that's happening" to intolerable really darn fast.

In addition to perhaps being hyposensitive (less sensitive than normal) to interoceptive feedback, people on the spectrum have difficulty filtering incoming sensory data from the environment. For example, when a typical person walks into an unfamiliar place, they quickly and instinctively filter out the unnecessary information to isolate important environmental data. In a doctor's office, they zero in on the reception desk. In a coffee shop, their brain immediately sorts out where the ordering line is. In a busy train station, they filter out the distractions to focus on the directional signs pointing to their platform.

If just reading about those unfamiliar situations raised your anxiety level, you're not alone. The autistic brain takes one look at the busy train platform and gives equal weight to the directional signs, the map on the wall, the crying toddler, the homeless man shaking his cup of coins, the stale underground smell, the roar of the trains, the sound of the bathroom hand dryer, the person brushing up against you, the uneven flooring, and countless other sights, sounds, smells, and physical sensations.

Like so many other things, what typical people do instinctively—filter out the sensory detritus to identify the relevant inputs—the Aspie brain does through a logical process of elimination. Given enough time, I can stand in the busy train station and find the correct directional signs, but it will usually take me longer than it would take most typical people.

So how does this apply to those everyday annoyances that we're so good at ignoring? Because we seem to receive so much of our environmental data at the same "volume" level, it's harder for any single piece of information to rise above the rest and get noticed. Typical people instinctively sort those same incoming signals by priority, so the "I'm too cold" signal gets mentally red flagged. This red flag message interrupts the part of the brain that's engaged in work to say, "Hey, we've got a problem over here."

The autistic brain doesn't seem to red flag sensory input until it reaches critical levels that make it physically impossible to ignore. By that point it's often too late, and a meltdown is imminent.

JUMPSTARTING THE PROCESS

If sensory hyposensitivity or sensory filtering challenges prevent you from noticing physical discomfort, I've found that there is a way to jumpstart the process:

Step 1: Be attentive to what your body is telling you. For me, the feeling that something is physically uncomfortable is very specific. It hovers right at the edge of my brain, like an itch that I can't quite reach. I try to listen for that feeling when I'm engaged in something else. The key to this step is recognizing the sensations that you have prior to reaching crisis level. When I first started working on this process, I spent a lot of time identifying the signal that means discomfort for me and then learning to listen for it. This can be the most difficult part of the process, but stick with it and keep mentally cataloging situations until you have a semi-reliable database of warning sensations to draw from.

Step 2: Consciously prioritize the feeling of discomfort as early as possible after you notice it occurring. For example, as I was about halfway through writing this, I started to get the itchy feeling that I've learned to recognize as my warning sensation. When I came to the end of a stream of thought I paused and disengaged my mind from writing to run a check of my body. I soon discovered the source of my discomfort: the sun was shining on my laptop monitor, creating a glare.

Step 3: Identify a solution. Is this a problem I can easily fix? How? In the case of the glare, I looked at the window beside me and discovered that there is a shade with a pull chain that will allow me to lower it. Sometimes the solution is very simple—a 30-second fix that will relieve the discomfort, allowing you to get back to whatever you were engrossed in. If the solution isn't immediately obvious, you may need to brainstorm or ask someone close by for assistance in solving the problem.

Step 4: Act on the problem. If the solution is simple, try to act on it right away. It can be hard to stop what you're doing to take that action, but once you do, you'll be able to concentrate better on your activity. I try to use that as an incentive to break away and do what I need to do. Again, if the solution is complex or seems too difficult to accomplish on your own, don't be afraid to ask for help or to engage in a rescue activity until you can manage the more complex steps needed. For example, if I get hungry to the point where making a meal feels impossible, I've found that eating a piece of fruit and drinking a big glass of water while relaxing in my favorite chair will boost my energy to the point where I feel up to the task of cooking or at least locating something more substantial to eat.

Don't be surprised if it takes a while to get the hang of addressing your physical discomfort before it reaches a crisis point. At least 15 minutes passed between the time I started to peripherally sense that something was wrong and the time I lowered the shade.

Learning coping strategies is hard work and requires patience. Rather than feeling bad because a typical person would spend about 15 seconds on a process that took me 15 minutes, I try to focus on the fact that a year ago, I would have just kept right on typing, squinting at the glare on my monitor and feeling miserable.

The Difference Between Procrastination and EF Fail

Some people might look at my example above and say, "That sounds like procrastination." For a long time I thought of myself as a chronic procrastinator. For example, there's a spot on my kitchen floor, a little cluster of dried reddish drips. I don't know what it is. If it's from three days ago, it's tomato sauce. If it's been there longer...who knows?

I've walked past it dozens of times. I look at it. It annoys me. I wonder how it got there. I wish it would go away. It doesn't occur to me that I can make that happen.

The greasy, smudgy fingerprints on the cabinet that I can only see in exactly the right light? The eight-inch long thread that's been hanging off the bathroom rug since the last vacuuming? The dryer sheet on the laundry room floor? Same thing.

What is this? Why can I sit here and catalog all of these little annoyances yet I still do nothing about them? It's not like fixing them would take a huge amount of time or effort.

In fact, to demonstrate how minor they are, I'll take care of them right now.

Done. It took me less than five minutes to wipe down the kitchen cabinets, trim the thread and toss it in the trash, pick up the dryer sheet, and clean the spot off the floor. I bet it would also take only a few minutes to vacuum up the bits of dirt and grass scattered in the entryway from my running shoes.

But I'm sitting here writing and not doing it, aren't I?

Maybe later.

And this is how days go by and I keep walking around the mess, getting more and more annoyed by its existence, yet still not doing anything about it.

PROCRASTINATION DOESN'T LOOK LIKE THIS

These things are so minor that I don't think avoiding them qualifies as procrastination. Look at some of the ways experts talk about procrastination:

- delaying a stressful task
- a way of coping with anxiety associated with starting or completing a task
- delaying an action despite expecting to be worse off
- may result in stress, guilt, crisis, severe loss of productivity, social disapproval
- impedes normal functioning
- issues of anxiety, low self-worth, self-defeating mentality, lack of confidence.

I can't say I have a whole lot of anxiety about my ability to spray some Windex on the floor and wipe up a spot. Loss of productivity because I'm not snipping that annoying thread off the bathroom rug? Probably not. If anyone actually came to my house, social disapproval might factor into the greasy finger smudges, but only in the sense that I'd be quick to clean them ahead of time.

I know procrastination when I see it. It involves a useless avoidance behavior, which I often talk myself into thinking is useful. "Instead of working on this really hard developmental editing project, I'm going to tag all of the files on my hard drive so they're easier to find!"

I recognize procrastination for what it is: my brain's way of avoiding a challenging task, or at least of working up to it.

Yet I don't go out of my way to do something in place of wiping up that spot on the floor. I just don't do it. It doesn't even occur to me to do it. My thought process is literally: "There's a spot on the floor. Huh. That's annoying. I wonder how it got there. Looks like sauce. Funny how it dripped in a circle like that. Wait, why did I come to the kitchen? Oh, right, there's an empty water glass in my hand."

That's what executive function impairment looks like when it comes to problem solving. Solving a problem, even a minor one, requires four EF-specific steps:

1. Identify the observed condition as a problem.
2. Plan a solution by selecting and ordering strategies.
3. Maintain strategies in short-term memory in order to perform them.
4. Evaluate the outcome and troubleshoot as necessary.

Steps 1 and 2 trip me up badly. My brain recognizes that there's a spot on the floor, but it doesn't necessarily identify it as a minor problem to be solved. Or it identifies it as a problem but doesn't realize that a solution is needed.

I've found a few helpful strategies for addressing difficulties with planning and problem solving:

- *Mindfulness*. In this case, mindfulness isn't some complex life practice. It's just a matter of realizing, "Oh, wait, I'm doing that thing again, which means I need to go get the vacuum/sponge/scissors and take care of this little annoyance that will only take a minute to fix and, oh, think how good I'll feel afterward."
- *Routines*. In the same way that routines can be helpful for getting everyday tasks done, they can work for problem solving too. For example, if I'm waiting for Sang to get ready to go out, I'll walk around our home, intentionally looking for little problems to take care of. Inevitably there will be a pile of clean laundry that needs folding or dishes that need to be picked up. This same routine works in the kitchen while waiting for something to boil or in the bathroom while waiting for the shower water to warm up.

- *Reminder software or apps.* There are many apps that will send you an email or phone alert for recurring household tasks. I have one that reminds me to wash the sheets every two weeks, trim the dog's toenails once a week and clean my car every three months. If there are some problems that occur regularly, try preempting them with scheduled reminders.

- *Strategic reminders.* Like the reminder apps, strategically placing visual reminders around the house can nudge you into acting on common problems. Leaving the vacuum in a high-traffic area not only reminds you to vacuum more often, but it makes it easier to get the job done because the tool you need is handy.

- *Use chunking.* If a problem gets to the point where you recognize that something needs to be done but the size of the task is now overwhelming, try breaking it into smaller parts. For example, instead of "cleaning your bedroom" start with a goal of getting everything off the floor or collecting the dirty laundry and washing it. As you tackle these smaller tasks, it will become more obvious what else is left to be done.

- *Ignore it!* Sometimes, simply ignoring minor problems is a solution in itself, especially if they'll get taken care of in the near future. For example, in the worst case, the spot on the floor would have gotten cleaned up during my regular biweekly house cleaning. If it's not posing a health hazard, maybe it doesn't need to get wiped up right now. Prioritizing and using energy wisely is an important part of problem solving.

There is one more place that problem solving can go wrong and that's staying on task. Sometimes I start to carry out a solution but get distracted and end up doing a completely different task. For example, I'll decide to fill out a form that requires me to find some information I have filed away, then realize that my filing system is out of whack, which leads to a complete reorganization of my filing cabinet. Two hours later I still haven't located the information I need, let alone filled out the form. My filing cabinet may look great, but that wasn't what I'd planned to do.

Impaired executive function leads to difficulty inhibiting behavior, making it hard to stay on task. It's easier to simply drift from task to task rather than sticking to a strategy for completing a more difficult chore. Planning aids like checklists and visual schedules can be helpful for staying on task if the activity is one that can be broken into logical steps. Following a series of specific steps and checking off each as you go prevents you from getting sidetracked—or at least from getting sidetracked for too long.

WHY TIME AGNOSIA MAKES PLANNING EVEN MORE DIFFICULT

Time agnosia, a common result of executive function impairment, is experienced as a lack of a sense of time. It can manifest as difficulty comprehending the order of events, how events fit together, and/or the duration of events.

Like other forms of EF impairment, there are workarounds that can lessen the impact of time agnosia on your daily life. For example:

- Ask someone to help you figure out how long common tasks or chores take so you can include enough time in your schedule for completing them.
- Make a list, note cards, or a visual schedule/aid showing the duration of common tasks and events for future reference.

- Draw visual blocks of time for each activity in relation to a reference activity with a duration that makes sense to you—for example, taking a shower = one third of a Doctor Who episode.
- Use tools like Google Maps to estimate travel times.
- Estimate how long complex tasks might take by breaking them down into smaller tasks. If you have to run three errands and pick up someone downtown at 4:00pm, start scheduling backwards, step by step. How long does it take to drive downtown from the last errand? How long will the last errand take (break it down really small if necessary: parking the car + walking into the store + plus finding an item + plus walking to the register, etc.)? How much time to drive from second errand to last errand? And so on, all the way back to the steps necessary for getting ready at home.

People with time agnosia are often very early or very late to events and have difficulty finishing things on time. Again, this is different from procrastination. They may want to get a project done on time but literally cannot figure out how to schedule the sequence of events needed to complete the task to coincide with the time that it's due.

A Final Word about Executive Function

We each have a limited amount of brain power we can devote to self-control and cognitive tasks in a given time period. If we devote energy to, for example, suppressing temptation, we'll be less willing to solve a difficult math problem or run an extra lap around the track.

Often referred to as ego depletion, this concept was first proposed by Roy Baumeister who did a series of landmark experiments to prove the link between self-control and our willingness to engage in difficult cognitive tasks. He found that people who were asked to resist eating chocolate cookies and candy were quicker to give up on solving challenging puzzles than those who were allowed to indulge in the sweets.

By now, you probably know enough about executive function to recognize that both tasks—inhibiting a behavior by not eating the tempting sweets and problem solving by completing challenging puzzles—are related to executive function.

Our brains don't differentiate between the EF required for inhibiting an enjoyable action or the EF required to solve a calculus problem. Every task that draws on our executive functioning capabilities eats up a little more of our limited supply. When you consider that autistic people start out with less executive function than typical people, it's easy to see why conserving EF resources can lead to better functioning in our daily lives.

There are a number of ways to conserve EF. Many of the life hacks discussed in this chapter—social scripts, routines, reminders, visual schedules—are ways to use less EF on simple tasks so that we have more left over for challenging activities like work or driving on a busy road.

There's one other way to conserve EF that you probably won't hear many people talk about: being your autistic self. Often, autistic people feel subtle—or not so subtle—social pressure to inhibit natural behaviors like stimming so they'll appear more "normal." This kind of pressure is not only emotionally damaging, it's cognitively counterproductive.

Think back to the experiment where the people who were told to resist eating chocolate gave up more easily on solving puzzles. Substitute stimming for chocolate and completing an important work project for solving puzzles. Factor in an autistic person's already impaired executive function, making inhibition of actions more challenging, and you can see why using up valuable EF resources to inhibit stimming can have a negative effect on our potential for working, going to school, and functioning on a daily basis.

In fact, I think this is why many autistic individuals find that they stim more when they're concentrating on a task. When we shift EF resources to problem solving or planning and away from behavior inhibition, our natural affinity for movement as a means of self-regulation becomes more evident. As we concentrate on the task, we may find ourselves fidgeting with a stim toy, bouncing a leg, flapping a hand, flexing our fingers, or rocking gently. While I'm working at the computer, I often find myself rhythmically tapping my fingers in sequence on my keyboard when I pause to think. Stimming on my keyboard helps me organize my thoughts and stay on task.

Of all the adaptations I've made in the past year to cope with my impaired executive function, allowing myself to stim more has been the easiest. At first I thought simply learning about EF and making the right adjustments would solve the problem but now I see that an executive function impairment never goes away. In fact, having impaired EF makes problem solving itself harder, which turns into a vicious cycle of "I could fix this if only I wasn't so broken."

In the end, I'm learning that the solution is a combination of making the adaptations that are realistic, seeking out supports where I need them and being kind to myself about the rest of it.

11

The Dark Side

There is a dark side to being autistic.

Before I knew about ASD and the complex ways it influences my life, I blamed myself for a lot of things—for being overly sensitive, easy to anger, controlling, anxious. I knew that I was prone to emotional breakdowns and periods of withdrawal, symptoms I associated with depression or emotional instability. Though I never sought treatment—probably because they were such a longstanding feature of my life—I knew that these things weren't "normal."

As I learned more about autism, I came to understand that growing up undiagnosed can leave us saddled with a lot of emotional baggage. Two of the heaviest loads I've carried into adulthood are a strong need for control and a secret sense of shame. The more obviously damaging of the two was my need for control.

Control sounds like a good thing.

Self-control. I've got this under control. Control yourself.

For years, I had everything under control. I swore I did. Everything from family activities to how people were allowed to feel around me. Is some small detail unplanned? I'll plan it. Someone has a problem? I'll fix it, whether they want me to or not. Something needs to be done? I'll take care of it. In fact, I'll do it myself because that's the only way it will get done right. Because only I know what the right way is.

See, everything under control.

This should feel good. My entire universe working according to my grand plan. Only it doesn't feel good. It's exhausting and it drives the people around me up a wall.

It's also an illusion.

How Do I Fix This?

When I started reading about Asperger's, one of the first things that "clicked" for me was why so much of my adult life was dominated by a need for control. I'm ill equipped for many aspects of life; at some point, control became my primary coping mechanism. Life was hard and confusing and scary. Being in control could fix that.

It doesn't, of course. If you've struggled to maintain an illusion of control, you know what I mean. Control strains and eventually suffocates relationships. It leaves you huddled in a corner, defending a small patch of territory that feels sacred. Sang says I latch onto the things that I see as mine, people included, and guard them. He says I need to possess things.

That's hard to hear, but he's right.

I've been that way for so long I don't remember if I was ever not like that. But until I had that key bit of information about *why* control was so important to me, it was something that lurked in the shadows, feeding a quiet sense of shame.

Changing something that's deeply ingrained on a subconscious level is hard. It happens in baby steps. When you're in the middle of it, nothing is as clearly defined as hindsight makes it appear. Looking back, I can see that understanding the root cause of the problem was the first step.

Step two was accepting that it *was* a problem. I didn't want to, at first. That meant admitting to myself that I'd hurt people so I could feel better. The hurt wasn't intentional, but it was damaging all the same. As I got braver, I was able to start examining what was triggering my need for control and then apply what I was learning about how my brain works to come up with new coping strategies.

Control was an all-purpose strategy. I couldn't just replace it with one new strategy. Instead, I had (and still have) to look at each situation and ask myself where is the urge to control this coming from? What will I need to feel safe or comfortable in this situation? How can that happen?

Sometimes there's a simple answer, like planning breaks into a long day of socializing. If I know that I can take a time out whenever I need one, the urge to control what everyone else is doing lessens. That was a big revelation for me: I can be in charge of me and everyone else is in charge of themselves.

THE BIG LEAP

The hard part about "everyone else is in charge of themselves" is that it requires me to trust other people so I can purposefully let go. Letting go is hard. When I let go, anything could happen. Someone could load the dishwasher wrong. Someone could be five minutes late for an appointment.

Someone could be sad in a way that I can't immediately fix.

Then what?

What I've realized is that controlling all those little details was my way of avoiding other types of discomfort. Disorder is uncomfortable. It doesn't matter if it's spatial, temporal, or emotional, major or minor. I wanted no part of it and I was going to do something about it.

I'm slowly letting go of that need.

Sometimes, even though I recognize that I need to step back from my urge to control, I still feel a strong need to *do something*. Then I remind myself that I am doing something: I'm respecting someone else's boundaries. I'm supporting them. I'm taking care of my needs rather than imposing that responsibility on another person.

Learning to manage my own internal distress is also making it easier for me to ask for what I need from others. My default internal cycle for many years was:

> *Panic → Lash out in a controlling way to make the panic stop*

When I first decided I wanted to change, the best I could manage was:

> *Panic → Question why I'm panicking → Who cares? → Lash out in a controlling way anyhow*

With practice, my new internal cycle is becoming:

> *Panic → Question why I'm panicking → Ask myself what I need to feel comfortable → Take steps to make that happen, including asking for help from others*

Ironically, the more I give up on trying to control all of the things and people around me, the less out of control I feel. And that really is a good thing.

Shame

While I was eager to confront my need for control and begin to change, it wasn't until the end of the first year after my diagnosis that I found the courage to talk about my shame. In fact, it was so hard for me to confront my feelings of shame that I had to sneak up on it, in the form of a conversation with myself:

"You've been putting off writing this for a while, haven't you?"

Yep.

"Weeks?"

More like months.

"And how's that working for you?"

Well, I wrote about functioning and the verbal–nonverbal disconnect and executive function to avoid what I really wanted to write about.

"Which is?"

Shame. All the things I'm *supposed* to be able to do. The ways executive function undermines developmental expectations. What it means to be independent and what it means to be developmentally delayed and why those two things are not mutually exclusive.

Because I don't live independently. I never have. I don't know if I could or not. I probably could if I had to, though maybe not as successfully as I'd like to pretend.

"You're doing it again, veering into an easier topic to avoid that shame thing a little longer."

Right. Shame. Hang on.

"Hey, enough with the Googling! Get back here and write something."

Relax. I needed context. How about this?

Shame is rooted in our perceived defects. When those defects are revealed to others, we see ourselves in a negative light. Shame creeps in.

"Yawn. Sounds like something you Googled. Try again."

Okay, okay. Here's an example of what I want to talk about:

If I don't shower for three days and there's no one around to notice, who cares? I got busy. I was distracted. My routine was thrown off. I forgot. It was too hot or too cold or too whatever.

I don't smell great, but no one has ever died of body odor and there's a simple remedy.

It's not a big deal to me. It's not a moral failing or laziness or a reflection on my ability to do other adult things. It's simply impaired executive function with a side order of sensory-processing issues.

"That's 300 words and only 24 of them are about shame so far. How, exactly, does the shame figure into this?"

The shame happens when someone else is around to notice that I haven't showered or brushed my hair or ironed my clothes or that I'm wearing the same shirt as yesterday, and oops it has a spot of last night's spaghetti sauce on the front.

Just writing that sentence has me cringing and wanting to delete it and trash this and never talk about this subject again.

"Worried about what the readers will think of you?"

Exactly. People are supposed to master self-care as a child or, at the latest, as a teenager. Not being able to accomplish basic self-care tasks consistently on a daily basis—and worse not noticing or seeming to care—suggests a certain lack of maturity. A lack of common sense, of intellectual development, or even of self-awareness.

I'd like to think I have all of those things, at least to the degree that the average adult does.

But I suspect others might see it differently. If you can't manage to brush and floss every day, how on earth will you manage complex tasks like paying bills, driving, or getting to work on time—let alone caring for another person, particularly a helpless little person?

"That does sound like a logical question."

I know, and I don't have a logical answer. It's not as if I don't know what self-care entails or can't execute the necessary steps required. It's not even that I'm intentionally not doing what is expected.

My self-care falls apart because it slides under the radar. This is going to sound unfathomable to the average adult, but I don't notice. For example, I shower as part of a daily routine: exercise then shower. On the days I don't exercise, I have to think about when to shower. Sometimes I keep thinking about it until dinner or bedtime. Sometimes I need to be prompted to go do it. If no one is around to do the prompting, well, the day could be gone—and I never shower before bed because that's somehow a rule—and that's that.

One day, two days, three days. It just happens.

"Maybe you need a minder."

I have one! The problem is, I'm married to him. How uncool—not to mention unromantic and unsexy and unequal-partnershipy is it when my husband needs to remind me to do all these little things? He's not my caretaker. It's not his responsibility—or at least I don't think it should be.

It's hard on a relationship when one partner has to assume a caretaking role at times. There's an element of "not what I signed up for" regardless of how generous and loving your partner is.

I'm lucky to be married to someone who gets it, who knows how to broach the subject in a nonchalant way or make just the right amount of a joke about it. But there are times—painful for both of us—when the thing at hand, the thing that's flying under my radar, is just a bit too much, too personal, too uncomfortable.

"So he doesn't tell you?"

Oh no, he tells me. He agonizes over whether he really needs to say something, but in the end he says it. I can tell by his voice, the way he starts the conversation, that what he's about to say is costing him. And those are the moments when I realize how strong our relationship is and how hard we've worked to get to this place. I appreciate that he loves me enough and is honest enough and brave enough and mature enough to say the hard things, the things that the average husband is not going to have say to his wife.

"You've written yourself into a corner again, haven't you?"

How can you tell?

"It's been four days since you opened this doc. That means you're dead in the water and this is going to end up being one of those pieces that never gets finished."

You're right, I was stuck. But I gave a draft to Sang. He read it—slowly, carefully, in the way that he reads whatever I hand him. Then he said, "Your sincerity and passion and discipline and all of your good qualities overshadow this other stuff for me." He said it's about care and that I deserve to have someone care for me.

I pushed a bit, asked him if he doesn't get tired of having to remind me about all those little things. He laughed and said, "Of course, but what am I going to do? We chose each other."

And suddenly everything seemed so simple.

What started out as a piece about shame has become a piece about love. Because where I look at myself and see executive dysfunction and shame and dependence, my husband looks at me and he sees what he always has: me.

"How nice for you."

What?

"I mean, that's great for you that you have such an understanding partner, but 'Go out and find an understanding partner' isn't exactly practical advice. And what about all the rest of it? The 'What will people think?' and the fact that you're still going to end up going three days without showering occasionally and..."

Okay, okay, I get it. I let myself get seduced by the guy I married. Again. He has a way of doing that. But I think there's a hint of a solution in that last realization. He accepts me as I am, even when I don't. He cares for me, even when I'm not sure I deserve it.

I'm hard on myself. Perhaps that's a coping mechanism. I scrutinize everything about myself down to the most minute details, because I so often discover after the fact that I've missed the obvious.

That might be where the shame is coming from, that feeling of failure, of not living up to some imaginary standard. I've always been prone to perfectionism, which I was surprised to learn is a common feature of ASD. Psychologists say that perfectionism is rooted in a desire to attain approval or love. It's also closely related to shame because perfectionists are constantly chased by the many *shoulds* in our lives.

Practically Perfect in Every Way

"You're such a perfectionist."

Are you cringing after reading that? I am.

Perfectionist is rarely used in a positive context. As a put down, it's a polite stand-in for rigid, controlling, procrastinating, slow, nitpicky, paralyzed. Even when people try to use it in a positive context, it rarely casts a favorable light.

I say this as a lifelong and unreformed perfectionist. And because I've been a perfectionist for as long as I can remember, I've given a lot of thought to the whys and hows of it. Perfectionism is believed to be rooted in childhood. We somehow get the idea in our heads that we're valued for our achievements. As we grow older, we base our self-worth on the approval of others, convinced that if we can do things perfectly, we'll be loved and accepted. If we fail, on the other hand, we must be worthless.

This is the classic explanation of perfectionism.

For me, the problem with this explanation is that I never quite felt like it fit. It's in the right ballpark. I do seek approval from others, though just as often I couldn't care less. I put a big emphasis in my life on my accomplishments. Doing well is important to me and I often believe there is a standard of perfection that I should live up to, or at least aim for.

What I don't fully see in myself is the worthlessness. I'm hard on myself when I fail, but I bounce back quickly. My fear of failure is low. I'm willing to put myself out there and see what happens, even when I know that the risk of failure is high. It's rare that I feel worthless, even when I screw up in a big way.

THE LINK BETWEEN AUTISM AND PERFECTIONISM

As I researched perfectionism, I came across more nuanced models. For example, some psychologists believe that there is adaptive perfectionism, which motivates us to strive for success without the negative impact on self-esteem that the classic maladaptive perfectionism carries.

Others classify multiple types of perfectionism based on the object of the perfectionistic thinking.

- *Self-oriented perfectionism*: setting irrationally high standards for one's own behavior, appearance, achievements, etc.
- *Other-oriented perfectionism*: setting irrationally high standards for others to conform to.
- *Socially prescribed perfectionism*: believing that others (particularly significant others) have irrationally high standards for one's self to conform to.

When perfectionism is broken down this way, I see myself in all three categories. But I think autistic perfectionism has some additional dimensions to it, beyond the classic model of, "If I'm perfect, people will love me."

First, our tendency toward black and white thinking can create an appearance of perfectionism. If I sit down to write an essay for English class with the idea that I will either produce the perfect essay or I will produce garbage, that looks a lot like perfectionism. But what if I think about my essay that way because I'm not good at thinking in shades of gray? What if it doesn't occur to me that between "perfect" and "garbage," there exists "pretty bad," "below average," "acceptable," "pretty good," "very good," "excellent," and "nearly perfect"?

It might seem like splitting hairs to differentiate between straight-up black and white thinking and perfectionism, but I think doing so can illuminate an important difference. If I'm trying to write the perfect essay because I truly think the only other option is a terrible essay, what I need to work on is remembering that there are other possibilities. If I'm trying to write the perfect essay because I think that doing anything less makes me a failure as a person, I need to work on my self-esteem.

Personally, I think my perfectionism is a mix of the two, weighted more toward black and white thinking, which may be why I don't have the pervasive feelings of worthlessness that commonly go along with perfectionism. If anything, I have the opposite problem. Often I'll finish something and think it *is* perfect, until someone tells me otherwise. I'm so certain that I haven't made a total disaster of it that the only other option is I've done a stunningly good job. Bizarrely, my perfectionism cuts both ways, again because I haven't accounted for things like "really well done" or "good enough" or "close but not quite" in my potential outcomes.

The other factor that feeds perfectionism in autistic people, I think, is rooted in our childhood experiences with failure. As I read through the questions on the Frost Multidimensional Perfectionism Scale, a questionnaire that measures perfectionism, I realized that my strong agreement with statements like, "I usually have doubts about the simple everyday things I do" and "People will probably think less of me if I make a mistake" is rooted in decades of living with undiagnosed ASD. Decades of knowing that something was off. Of feeling like I had to work a lot harder than other people to keep up a semblance of normalcy. Of trying to hide all the little ways in which I not only wasn't perfect, but I wasn't even "normal."

Passing, after all, is a kind of perfectionism in itself. It may even be possible to make an argument that our subconscious need for approval is an upshot of the pressure to pass that we feel from childhood. Autistic perfectionism is like the deluxe bonus edition of perfectionism: subconscious need for approval plus black and white thinking plus social/internal pressure to pass. And like a lot of deluxe bonus editions, this one isn't really worth paying extra for.

THINKING IN ABSOLUTES

Not all autistic individuals are perfectionists, but most of us tend to think in absolutes. Either I'm great at something or I'm a failure. I'm going to get to my job interview on time and everything will be fine or I'm going to be late and everything will be ruined.

In reality, there are other options. I might get to my job interview on time only to discover it's been canceled. I might get there five minutes late and make a bad first impression, but win over the interviewer with my qualifications and preparedness. Or I might arrive a few minutes late to find that the interviewer is still in a meeting and not ready for me yet anyhow.

The tendency to leap to the worst possible conclusion—the "everything will be ruined" option—is known as catastrophizing. Like perfectionism, it's a common trait of ASD and closely tied to black and white thinking.

Sometimes catastrophizing can be useful. For example, running through all of the minor things that might go wrong with a job interview can be a way to plan for or preempt possible problems. Developing scripts and contingency options will make you more likely to succeed than not thinking about the interview and having to wing it when something unexpected comes up.

One way I've found to reduce the perseverative aspect of minor catastrophizing is making notes, lists, and schedules to reduce the amount of information in my head. As I write down each aspect of a plan, I tell myself that I've dealt with that potential outcome and now I can move on.

Minor catastrophizing, whether it's useful or simply annoying, isn't so bad. It's certainly not detrimental to my psyche like serious catastrophizing is. The serious type starts out small—like a case of poison ivy starts with one little itchy bump—and gradually creeps up on me until I find myself taking a sledgehammer to my self-esteem.

Serious catastrophizing for me is nearly always tied to social interaction. For example, there was a conference last summer for autistic adults. I didn't register for the conference initially because it felt, as odd as this sounds, like something other people do. I'd only just begun thinking of myself as autistic, after all. When I saw people that I know online making plans, I realized that it was something I'd like to do, but there was the practical barrier of it being too late to attend.

Then, somehow, I completely forgot about the logistical reasons for not going and turned it into, "I must be a freak because I can't do what everyone else is doing. What's wrong with me? I'm a terrible failure of a human being." Which isn't true. When I write that and read it back, I know it's not true. And yet that feeling lingered for a long time.

I don't know why autistic people are so prone to thinking in absolutes. Combine that with our superhero-level perseveration skills and the combination can be rough on the self-esteem. I've been trying for a while to dial back the catastrophizing but it feels like an intractable problem. Even that feeling is probably catastrophizing.

I have been able to sort out some of the components of catastrophizing to try to better understand what's happening:

- *Catastrophizing is illogical.* It leads to dire future predictions *based on something that hasn't even happened yet.* If X happens then the dreadful Y will happen, which will lead to the even more horrible Z. But look at the first word in that sentence: "If." X hasn't happened yet and there's no guarantee it will, so why the heck am I already worrying about Z!? Logically (and statistically) the odds of X, Y, Z happening are much smaller than the odds of X happening. And X hasn't happened yet.

- *Catastrophizing sets up a false choice.* Thinking in absolutes creates a false choice between only two alternatives: a great one and an awful one. In reality there are many possible outcomes between "Everything is perfect" and "Everything is terrible."

- *Catastrophizing poisons the water.* Autistic individuals are supposed to be bad at generalizing but when it comes to catastrophizing, we're experts. "I did this bad thing, ergo I must be a bad person." No. Good people do bad things. Good people screw up or are too scared to do things. You can be unhappy with something you've done while still being happy with yourself overall.

- *Catastrophizing thrives on inaction.* Thinking, thinking, thinking. That's what catastrophizing is, right? A bunch of thoughts, one worse than the next, feeding off each other. One way to stop them is to take action. Do something distracting. Call up that friend and find out if she really hates you or she's just been too busy to ring you. Treat yourself to a triple chocolate cupcake. Do something, anything, to get out of that rut of thinking, thinking, thinking.

- *Catastrophizing can be a proxy.* Sometimes unrelated anxiety, fears, or vulnerabilities feed catastrophizing. Anxiety about an upcoming job interview gets expressed as obsessive thoughts about an uncertain romantic relationship or an aging pet's health. Is the thing you're catastrophizing about really your biggest concern or is it a handy distraction?

- *Catastrophizing is an emotional magnet.* It attracts negative energy and holds it in place. The things we catastrophize about are often the weakest link in our emotional universe. For me, my social skills are my weak link. If I'm in major catastrophizing mode, it most likely involves my ability to relate to other people.

- *Catastrophizing thrives in secret.* It's hard to catastrophize out loud because it's such an irrational act. The minute I say, "I'm a failure at being a person" to someone else, they're going to poke all kinds of holes in that statement. But in my head, I can keep reinforcing the negativity ad infinitum.

- *Catastrophizing is rewarding.* This is confusing because I don't understand how such a maladaptive, self-destructive habit is so self-reinforcing. Maybe it's a way of preempting the worst-case scenario? Maybe it's because self-pity feels good? Maybe it feels like creating certainty in an uncertain situation, even if that certainty is an awful one? I don't understand why, but catastrophizing has a self-soothing effect, even as it makes me feel terrible.

It's that last point that blows all the rest out of the water. I can look at all the logical reasons that I've listed to justify how detrimental and unproductive catastrophizing is, but then I get to the last point and I'm right back where I started.

In some way, catastrophizing might be a way of tricking myself into feeling okay with comforting myself. If I leap to the conclusion that something awful will happen, I can then comfort myself, all the while telling myself that the comfort is well deserved. Perhaps one of the answers to cutting the cycle of catastrophizing short is to recognize it as a sign that I'm in need of self-soothing and go directly to practicing self-care in a healthy way rather than backing myself into it by administering a beating to my self-esteem first.

Often, a bad cycle of catastrophizing will send me into a period of withdrawal, another aspect of autism that is part of the dark side.

Withdrawal/Shutdown

Withdrawal. Shutdown. People on the spectrum use different words for the disappearing act we perform under stress. Sensory input becomes too much. Too many people, too much noise, too many decisions, too little time to process it all. We withdraw into ourselves, temporarily shutting out the overwhelming input.

I've learned to recognize the signs of withdrawal. The first is a sudden heavy sleepiness. All I want to do is put my head down and close my eyes. Or better yet, curl up in a nice safe place and take a nap. Of course, the urge to withdraw almost always hits at a time when a nap is impossible and there are no safe places nearby.

The second sign—the one that makes it clear I'm not just overtired—is the sensation of moving through a long tunnel. Everything around me recedes and grows quieter. I feel myself disconnecting from the people around me. It becomes harder to formulate responses and I have no motivation to initiate any interaction.

Once I've drifted far enough into the tunnel, I'm content to sit and stare off into space, detached from everything that's happening around me. I feel invisible.

COMMON SIGNS OF WITHDRAWAL OR SHUTDOWN
• Becoming less verbal or nonverbal. • Looking "spaced out" or detached from what's happening. • Staring at a fixed point in space. • Responding to direct inquiries with one-word answers or not at all. • Withdrawing from social spaces, not wanting to be around people. • Curling up in the fetal position. • Hiding under furniture, blankets, etc.

My withdrawals are almost always triggered by cumulative stress, and not always of the negative type.

One memorable withdrawal took place during an otherwise enjoyable weekend at the beach. The morning leading up to the withdrawal was marked by a series of minor frustrations. On any other day, I would have simply rolled with them, but two days of being in an unfamiliar environment had silently taken its toll.

Suddenly, at lunchtime, the music in the restaurant was too loud, the sun was too bright, I couldn't tune out the conversations at the tables around me, the menu had too many options, none of which looked good. Sitting half in the sun and half in the shade, I was too cold and too hot at the same time. Every time I looked up, the guy at the next table quickly looked away—and I think that was the last straw.

I frequently catch people staring at me, often repeatedly over the course of a meal or a train ride and I'm not sure why. Off went my perseverative brain, puzzling over that question and then—bam—the sleepiness rolled in and next thing I knew I was slipping into the tunnel.

GOING OFFLINE

Contrary to how it must look externally, when I'm withdrawn I'm not sad or depressed. Sometimes a withdrawal is triggered by anxiety but sometimes it's triggered by having too much fun. Whatever the trigger, a withdrawal is always the result of being overwhelmed.

Once I've disappeared, though, the dominant feeling is one of comfortable blankness. Relief.

Withdrawing or shutting down is a defense mechanism. My brain decides that the processing demands of my environment have become too high and it takes some resources offline for a while. The withdrawal itself is restorative, a sensory time out, but it's not voluntary and even when I know it's happening, there's little I can do to stop or control it.

Do I need to control it? Do I want to? Ideally, it would be nice to delay a withdrawal to a more convenient time, like during the drive home instead of in the middle of lunch. But the urge to withdraw is strong and physical, more like being hungry than being sad. I can talk myself out of being sad, but being hungry only goes away if I eat something.

Looking at a withdrawal as a physical need makes it easier to see that it's not something I can simply distract myself from. Still, it's hard to accept feeling helplessly ruled by my body. Ultimately, I think, the answer lies in what comes before the withdrawal, that series of little frustrations made worse by being out of my element.

I'm getting better at managing unexpected change. I'm slowly learning to embrace the unfamiliar. I'm becoming more mindful of the ways my physical comfort affects my emotional shifts. But perhaps I'm still too good at stuffing down the negative emotions, the little discomforts and anxieties that don't feel important enough to waste energy on.

RESURFACING

Normally, if someone tries to engage me in conversation when I've shut down, all they get are monosyllabic answers. When I had that lunchtime withdrawal on vacation, Sang asked, "Where are you?" My nonanswer was "Why?"

He paused a moment, probably wondering if he was doing the right thing by confronting the situation head-on and then he said, "You disappeared."

That simple acknowledgment of what I was experiencing helped me re-engage with him. We'd never talked about my withdrawals before. We'd also never talked about their darker cousins, my meltdowns. I think Sang has always assumed they were all simply bad moods, something to be ridden out and ignored. Finally, talking about my shutdowns opened the door for me to write about my meltdowns, which are far more unpleasant.

Meltdowns

One day, right after a particularly bad meltdown, I decided to attempt to capture my thoughts and feelings because when I have a meltdown I have difficulty speaking and can't explain verbally how I'm feeling or why.

I'm going to reproduce those unedited thoughts here, exactly as I wrote them immediately after the meltdown, in the hope that they will be helpful to others who want to understand what a meltdown feels like. I'd like to preface the raw thoughts that follow with a caveat about what it means to lose control during a meltdown.

During a meltdown, I lose control of my emotional regulation and my communication faculties, but I don't lose control of my behavior toward others. Even though I have difficulty communicating complex concepts during a meltdown, I still understand what is morally and socially acceptable. I might cry uncontrollably, curl up in a ball, become unable to speak, engage in self-harming stims or kick an inanimate object, but I've never had the urge to harm another person. I have occasionally harmed myself (as you'll read in the passage that follows) though never in a way that did permanent damage.

ANATOMY OF A MELTDOWN

A meltdown can go one of two ways:

Explosion: Everything flies outward. Words. Fists. Objects.

Implosion: Have you ever seen a building implode? The charges go off somewhere deep inside and for a moment you swear nothing is going to happen and then seconds later—rubble and dust and a big gaping hole in the ground.

It feels like a rubber band pulled to the snapping point.

What I don't want to hear:

"It's okay." [It's not.]

"You need to pull yourself together." [I will, when I'm ready.]

"Everything will be fine." [I know.]

I'm not looking at you because I don't want to see you seeing me this way.

It feels like the end of the world. It feels like nothing will ever be right again.

What I need:

- space
- time
- absence of judgment.

The headbanging impulse is intermittent but strong. I stave it off as best I can because:

- my brain is not an infinitely renewable resource
- headbanging scares other people.

Meltdowns are necessary. Cleansing. An emotional purge. A neurological reboot.

Please don't ask me if I want to talk about it, because:

- there's nothing to talk about
- I don't have the resources necessary for talking.

Evolution of meltdowns over a lifetime:

For my first 12 years, I internalize well. So well that I end up in doctors' offices and emergency rooms with mysterious headaches, high fevers, stiff necks, and stomach bugs. At various times I'm told that I don't have meningitis, migraines, appendicitis. What I do have...that's never conclusively decided. Things come and go, seemingly without rhyme or reason.

Puberty hits. Hormone surges make internalizing impossible. I slam doors, sob uncontrollably at the slightest provocation, storm out of the house, crank up my stereo. My anger becomes explosive. I pinball between implosions and explosions.

Early 20s, into my 30s, the explosions become rare but the implosions grow worse. I can't get through an emotionally charged conversation with my husband—let alone a fight—without imploding. The headbanging impulse appears. Muteness takes center stage.

My 40s—I can count the explosions on one hand. The implosions are down to a few a year at most. As the meltdowns have lessened, the shutdowns have increased. This is lateral movement, not progress.

It feels like my whole body is thrumming, humming, singing, quivering. A rail just before the train arrives. A plucked string. A live wire throwing off electricity, charging the night air.

I'm 90 percent successful at staving off headbanging. The thing is: when that impulse arises, headbanging feels good. It's...fulfilling?

"Will comforting me help?" [No.]

"Do I want the meltdown to be over?" [Yes, but not prematurely.]

"Would I like a hug?" [No.]

"Am I in danger?" [No. I'm conscious of the boundary between stimming and serious self-harm.]

"Do I want company?" [If you're okay with sitting silently beside me.]

"Can you do anything to make me feel better?" [Probably not. But you can avoid doing the things that will make it worse.]

Muteness: Complex speech feels impossible. There is an intense pressure in my head, suppressing the initiation of speech, suppressing the formation of language.

There is a tipping point. My meltdowns aren't so much about triggers as thresholds. A mental red zone. Once I cross into that zone, there's no going back.

It feels like dropping a watermelon on the pavement on a hot summer day. The bobble, the slip, the momentary suspension of time just before the hard rind ruptures and spills its fruit, sad and messy, suddenly unpalatable. And no one knows whether to clean it up or just walk around it.

A shutdown is a meltdown that never reached threshold level. Either my threshold is rising or I'm becoming less sensitive to triggers as I age.

Meltdowns are embarrassing. They are a total loss of control. They are humiliating. They make me feel like a child. They are raw, unfiltered exposure.

Panic. Helplessness. Fear.

Imagine running as far as you can, as fast as you can. When you stop, *that feeling*—the utter relief, the exhaustion, the desperate need for air, the way you gulp it in, your whole body focused on expanding and contracting your lungs—that's what crying feels like during a meltdown.

Please don't touch me. Don't try to pick me up, move me, or get me to change positions. Whatever position I've ended up in is one that's making me feel safe. If it makes you uncomfortable to see me curled up in a ball on the floor, you should move—remove yourself from the situation.

There is emotion at the starting line, but a meltdown is a physical phenomenon: the racing heart. The shivering. The uncontrollable sobs. The urge to curl up and disappear. The headbanging. The need to hide. The craving for deep pressure. The feeling of paralysis in my tongue and throat. The cold sweat.

The physical cascade needs to run its course. Interrupt and it'll just start all over again a few minutes later. Patience, patience.

What I need when I'm winding down:

- deep pressure
- quiet
- understanding
- to pretend it never happened.

The recovery period is unstable.

Exhaustion comes first. Mixed with anger, at myself mostly, for losing control.

My filters don't come back online right away. Unless you can handle an unfiltered Aspie, proceed with caution.

Finally, there is euphoria. A wide open feeling of lightness, of soaring, of calm.

WHY MELTDOWNS HAPPEN

Like shutdowns and withdrawals, meltdowns are the consequence of a series of triggers—the first or worst of which might have occurred quite some time ago. A meltdown isn't necessarily triggered by a big emotional upset. Many times, the situation that appears to be the trigger is simply the final straw in a chain of triggers.

When it comes to meltdowns, I've learned that I have a point of no return. Up until that point, I can head off a meltdown. I'll pay for it, probably in the form of being unusually short-tempered, less able to function, exhausted or maybe shutting down. Past the point of no return, though, even if I can stop the meltdown from happening temporarily—for example, because I'm in a public place—it will eventually happen. I might be able to put it off for a few hours or overnight, but it's going to happen.

Once I've passed my point of no return, the meltdown is not only inevitable, but necessary to getting past the upsetting feelings that the triggering event has provoked. One of the most important things to remember about shutdowns, withdrawals, and meltdowns is that they are not (usually) voluntary occurrences. They happen, whether we want them to or not, because life has become overwhelming.

We withdraw or shut down in self-defense. We melt down because it's the only way to release the intense build-up of energy in our bodies and brains.

Meltdowns are hard on everyone. The autistic person experiencing the meltdown often feels bad for losing control, and family members or friends feel distressed at not being able to help much. My husband is the only person who has ever seen me have a meltdown as an adult, and for many years, he found them frustrating and painful to witness.

Talking and writing about my meltdowns and withdrawals—what they are, why they happen, and what they feel like—has helped him understand them better. That understanding makes it easier on him because he knows that I'm not expecting him to fix the situation, that he probably hasn't done anything to cause it, and that there's not much he can do to make me feel better until the worst has passed. It also makes it easier on me because he is better able to support me until I'm ready to talk about what's happened.

HELPING SOMEONE THROUGH A SHUTDOWN, WITHDRAWAL, OR MELTDOWN

Withdrawals, shutdowns, and meltdowns can be as stressful to watch as to experience. What can loved ones or friends do to help?

- Be quietly and calmly supportive.
- Ask if there is any way you can help.
- If there isn't, accept it and be patient.
- Don't impose your ideas of what the other person needs on them.

12

Redefining Myself

A funny thing happens when you're given a label. Suddenly that label seems to define everything you are. There's a famous Zen saying:

> Before I studied Zen, mountains were mountains, and water was water. After studying Zen for some time, mountains were no longer mountains, and water was no longer water. But now, after studying Zen longer, mountains are just mountains, and water is just water. (Ch'ing-yüan Wei-hsin)

An autism diagnosis is a lot like this. Inevitably, there is *Before* and *After*.

Before, I was me and Asperger's was Asperger's. My thoughts and actions were shaped by my personality, my upbringing, my environment, and my choices. I thought of them as my own. Asperger's Syndrome was something that described other people.

After receiving my diagnosis, I was no longer me and Asperger's was no longer a label applied to others. Suddenly, I was Asperger's and Asperger's was me.

After, everything I do, say, think, feel, experience is Aspergerized. Exhausted after a long shopping excursion? Sensory overload. Tripped and fell while running? Motor skills deficit. Didn't think to send my daughter the title to her car when she told me she was selling it? Poor executive function.

In the months following my diagnosis, "I'm an Aspie" became my default explanation. I no longer knew where Asperger's ended and I began—yet I constantly attributed my actions, thoughts, and behaviors to this separate thing called Asperger's.

Finding the Right Labels

Soon I was confronted with other labels: "autistic," "disabled," "high functioning." I was faced with the questions of what it means to have a disorder and whether "normal" even exists.

The "Asperger's" label was one that I had welcomed immediately—it felt like a good fit and it was my official diagnosis. "Autistic" was a harder label to accept. I'd always thought of autistic people as nonverbal and cut off from the world. I now realize that I'd bought into a dangerous stereotype.

As part of the online autistic community, I learned a lot about labels. I've learned that the autism spectrum is as diverse as the neurotypical spectrum. I've learned that speaking is not the only means of communicating with the world around us. I've learned that the autism spectrum is not hierarchical; we can't quantify the people on it using neatly bounded phrases or concepts.

I now proudly call myself autistic.

"Disabled" was the hardest to reconcile. The dictionary definition for disabled is: "A physical or mental condition that limits a person's movements, senses, or activities."

Undeniably, yes, that applies to me. Autism is a neurological (physical) condition that limits (or at least alters the function of) my senses and my activities to varying degrees. Still I struggled with the "disabled" label. My resistance had nothing to do with the appropriateness of a dictionary definition and everything to do with my biases against the negative connotation of the label.

It wasn't until I discovered the social model of disability that I was able to make my peace with the "disabled" label. The traditional model of disability—the medical model—looks at a disabled person's body as something that is broken and needs to be fixed. The social model points to the way society is organized as the limiting factor for disabled people. Removing barriers like negative attitudes toward disabled people and a lack of supports and adaptations are the focus of the social model.

So yes, I am disabled. Many of my autistic traits make life harder for me than it is for the average person. But in thinking about how my life is different because of ASD, I've also realized that some of my autistic traits are double-edge swords, simultaneously gifting me with strengths and challenges. Impaired perspective taking? It makes it harder for me to work out people's intentions but it also makes me nonjudgmental. Trouble with generalizing? That means I have to learn a similar lesson many times over, but gifts me with a dogged optimism and unconventional problem-solving skills.

Other strengths are actually coping mechanisms in disguise, skills that I've overdeveloped to survive in a neurotypical world. Being autistic has made me a survivor—forced me to adapt, by choice and necessity. The result is a unique set of strengths. As I've redefined myself, taking on sometimes difficult and life-altering labels, I found a strong need to celebrate my strengths too. So, in no particular order, here they are:

- I'm *nonjudgmental*. I take people at face value and will give someone the benefit of the doubt until they prove me wrong. A lifetime of being judged on appearance and first impressions will do that to you, I suppose.

- I have a *strong attachment to the truth*. Telling it. Seeking it. Hearing it. I value honesty above many other traits—probably because I'm so bad at detecting dishonesty.

If you ask me a question, you'll get an honest answer. Perhaps more honest than you'd like.

- I'm *curious*. Insatiably so. I love learning, discovering, knowing. My need for knowledge feels limitless, exciting, and empowering. Give me an answer and I'll have a handful of questions in reply.

- I'm *loyal*. My attachments to people are few, but when I do form a bond with someone it's a strong one. I will stand up for the people I care about in the face of a great deal of opposition.

- I'm *sincere*. Perhaps naively so. When I do something for another person, I do it wholeheartedly. People often seem puzzled by my sincerity, disbelieving, as if being sincere is some elaborate form of manipulation.

- I have a *well-defined set of values*. The black and white thinking of Asperger's means that I've developed a clearly delimited value system. This can be a blessing and a curse. There is a thin line between being principled and being stubbornly dogmatic. At most times, though, my values are my compass and my rudder, helping me navigate the ambiguities of a neurotypical world.

- I'm an *unconventional problem solver*. I'm not afraid to ask wild questions or examine solutions that appear to have little hope of working. My instincts can get way ahead of my ability to verbalize them. Often, I'm told that things won't work or don't make sense—right up until I go ahead and do what I have in mind and it works. Or doesn't. It's a crapshoot, but that does little to dent my confidence and willingness to try.

- I'm an *optimist*. I live in the here and now. I have few regrets. I view situations starting from zero. Aspies aren't very good at generalizing from one occurrence to another similar occurrence, which I think leads to an irrational level of optimism. Sure, something went wrong in the past, but (my brain always seems to say) this time will be different. Sometimes it is. Either way, I've found that taking an optimistic view of life makes me happy.

WHAT ARE YOUR STRENGTHS AND SUPERPOWERS?

Here are some descriptors of traits and abilities often associated with people on the spectrum:

- reliable
- honest
- nonjudgmental
- free of social expectations
- accepting of those who are different
- detail oriented
- accurate
- focused
- persistent
- good endurance
- able to deeply engage with a subject
- conscientious
- enthusiastic about beloved subjects/activities
- often excel in one area
- sincere
- guileless
- independent minded

- individualistic
- principled
- original or out-the-box thinkers
- knowledgeable
- hard workers
- dependable
- loyal
- better than average memory
- good pattern recognizers
- present in the moment
- analytical
- good at amusing themselves
- excel at individual sports or pastimes
- have strong values
- enjoy learning
- good at research
- truth seeking
- unconventional sense of humor
- creative
- visual thinker
- good at creating systems or methods of organizing large amounts of information
- intrinsically motivated
- appreciate the details of an environment
- creative problem solvers
- logical
- calm in a crisis.

MY AUTISTIC SUPERPOWERS (OR HOW ASD HAS MADE ME WHO I AM)

One of the myths of Asperger's is that all Aspies are savants—that we're born with some profound skill, like the ability to name the day of the week for any date in history, draw the New York subway system from memory, or do complex mathematical calculations in our heads.

Some autistic people *are* savants, but sadly, I have no savant skills. I've always been fascinated by people who do. I think it would be amazing to have a photographic memory or to instinctively understand mathematical systems.

Like a lot of Aspies, I do have a few overly developed traits. Though they aren't at the level of a savant skill, I've started to think of them as my autistic superpowers. They're the things about me that people comment on as being out of the ordinary or above average. They're a significant part of my self-identity:

- I'm *detail oriented*. I notice everything: changes and irregularities, patterns, and habits. I can analyze the hell out of things. I see patterns where most people don't. My affinity for details began as a coping mechanism—a way to identify patterns in social situations that I couldn't work out instinctively. Now it's become my default mode for making sense of the world around me.

- I'm *calm in a crisis*. If something goes wrong, I have an almost superhuman ability to separate myself from the situation and think clearly. My instinct is to focus on the facts at hand and retain an emotional detachment in situations where others get overwhelmed by panic.

- I'm *dependable* and *disciplined*. Both of these have roots in my need for routine. Once I get a routine in place, I can do the same thing without tiring of it. I can keep the books, walk the dog, sort the mail—day after day, like clockwork—as long as it's part of my daily schedule. I'm the kind of person people rely on. I get things done.

- I'm *determined*. Perseveration has a huge upside. If a problem or task catches my attention, I'll go at it like a Doberman with a ragdoll. I'll work at something long past the time when a more rational person would throw in the towel. A big part of success for me is simply not giving up too soon.

I can try to quantify how my autistic nature contributes to my strengths, just as I can hypothesize how it contributes to my weaknesses, but ultimately the line between my autistic traits and my other more typical personality traits is fuzzy. It's impossible to separate me from autism in the same way that it's impossible to categorize my autism using a label like "high functioning."

Aspies are often labeled high functioning by default. Some people even seem to think it's a compliment.

"You must be very high functioning. You don't seem autistic."

"Why, thank you. And you're not especially ugly."

High functioning is the one label I've rejected.

Functioning Labels in Practice

Applying functioning labels to autistic people is problematic. Maybe an example will help illustrate why.

I'll describe two autistic women, Mary and Joan. See if you can tell which one is high functioning and which one is low functioning.

Mary is a wife and mother. She's been steadily employed since age 16, has a BA degree and runs her own small business. She exercises regularly and is health conscious. When her daughter was younger, she volunteered for parent committees, hosted sleepovers, coached softball, and drove carpool. As the more detail-oriented spouse, Mary has always managed the family finances and investments. She has a diverse set of hobbies and pastimes that include dog training, target shooting, reading mystery novels, and fiction writing.

Joan is a wife and mother too. Her marriage has been rocky at times, thanks to her undiagnosed ASD, and she has no close friends. Joan works at home, avoids speaking to people on the phone and prefers to spend most of her days alone. Joan sometimes needs to be reminded to brush her hair, shower, or put on appropriate clothing before going out. She's never negotiated a lease or car purchase by herself and has never lived on her own. She enjoys going to the zoo, vacations at Disney World, watches animated movies, and she has several stuffed animals that she likes to cuddle up with after a hard day.

It's obvious that Mary is high functioning and Joan is low functioning, right?

What if I told you that Mary and Joan are the same person—that I created Mary and Joan by selectively using aspects of myself to construct two polarized versions of me? I am all of those things—high functioning one moment and low functioning the next.

A NONUNIFORM SET OF COMPETENCIES

One of the central problems of functioning labels is that they presume a uniform set of competencies. Just as neurotypical people aren't uniformly skilled at everything, autistic people have varying levels of competence in different areas of our lives. For some of us, these levels can be incongruously varied. They can shift over time, meaning that we might appear to be very competent in one area today and much less so a month later.

Driving is a good example. Some autistic people drive and some don't. Some learn to drive later in life and some as teenagers. I learned to drive at 15 and got my license the week I turned 16. I'm a good driver but I've learned that there are times when I need to be extra careful. If I'm overloaded, my ability to take in all the information required to drive safely is diminished. I'll do an apparently careless thing like drive over a curb and back into a parked car (or a telephone pole or a payphone).

Most of the time I'm a high-functioning driver. Sometimes I'm not. I've learned how to recognize when I might not be at my best and make allowances.

FUNCTIONING IS NONLINEAR

The subtle implication in "high functioning" is often "not that defective."

I understand the urge to want to signal "not that bad." Autism carries stigma. Simply saying, "I'm autistic" can be stigmatizing. That's a fact of life and one we can't escape. So people say high functioning as a way to lessen their discomfort.

But there's a danger of others hearing high functioning, with its "not that defective" undertones, and equating it with "doesn't need supports or services or accommodations or even any sort of understanding or acceptance."

If you're high functioning, you must be fine, right? You don't really need a little extra time to complete your work or to get instructions in writing or to sit in a quiet place so you can concentrate. You can just high function your way around all those little problems and get stuff done like a normal person.

Because if you're high functioning, you're practically normal! So close to normal. So, so close.

If only you would work a little harder and get the rest of your functioning ducks in a row, you'd be all set. And then the question becomes, why aren't you doing that? Or why are you suddenly backsliding? We fixed this thing and that thing and the other thing already. Why is it a problem all over again?

Just as functioning isn't uniform, it isn't linear either. There is a commonly seen phenomenon in autistic children where they'll make big gains in elementary school then regress when they hit adolescence. Or a child will be labeled a late bloomer, seeming practically "normal" in their teen years, then seem to backslide dramatically when they go off to college or enter the adult world of work and independent living.

The idea of backsliding or regressing implies that the executive function deficits, sensory sensitivities, and other cognitive differences that come with ASD can be fixed, like a broken leg. Parents and others are surprised when, after the metaphorical cast has been off for years, their child suddenly starts limping again.

What they don't see is that life has delivered a metaphorical baseball bat to the kneecaps.

Those kids or teens or adults who appear to have improved their functioning have in fact found coping mechanisms and adaptations. They haven't changed the underlying differences in their neurology. When the demands of life outstrip those coping mechanisms or adaptations, the underlying difficulties resurface. This isn't a cause for alarm. It simply means that new coping mechanisms, supports, or adaptations need to be found.

Functioning is fluid, nonlinear, and nonuniform.

Am I Disordered?

There is another label that I was given that I disagree with. When I was diagnosed with Asperger's, I was also diagnosed with an anxiety disorder.

Here's how I feel about that: "Social anxiety?" Yes. "Disorder?" Not so much.

Disorder implies that my social anxiety is irrational. Is it? Consider this:

> Anxiety at appropriate levels is important for adaptive functioning. There are many environmental hazards that must be avoided and these are often learned through the process of anxiety induction. The resultant anxiety response is learned through the association of certain stimuli with unpleasant consequences. (Romanczyk and Gillis)[1]

Anxiety, like fear, protects us from danger. It raises our guard and makes us wary. In this way, it's healthy. Without it, we might be less motivated to get an education, to work, to care for our loved ones and ourselves.

WHAT IS ANXIETY?

Anxiety is a state of worry, concern, or dread related to something that hasn't yet happened and may, in fact, never happen. Think about some things that we typically feel anxious about:

- committing to a relationship
- giving a major presentation for school or work
- becoming a parent
- meeting a partner's family
- starting a new job

---

1 R.G. Romanczyk and J.M. Gillis (2006) "Autism and the Physiology of Stress and Anxiety" in M.G. Baron, J. Groden, G. Groden, and L.P. Lipsitt (eds) *Stress and Coping in Autism*. New York: Oxford University Press, p.186.

- learning to drive
- flying on an airplane for the first time
- traveling in a high-crime area.

When you feel anxious about an upcoming event, you spend more time thinking about it and preparing for it than you would for a more mundane activity. You examine the possible consequences and give extra attention to your actions to ensure the best possible outcome. Anxiety heightens your awareness; heightened awareness sharpens your focus, increasing your safety.

It's important to note that when I talk about anxiety, I'm referring to appropriate levels of anxiety, not paralyzing anxiety. An appropriate level of anxiety is one that is manageable. I feel nervous in the days before giving an important presentation, but I manage my anxiety and complete the presentation to the best of my ability. An inappropriate level of anxiety is one that prevents a person from completing a necessary or desired activity. For example, if I got so anxious about the presentation that I ended up sick in bed, fainted in the conference room, or lied to avoid presenting, that would be a sign that my anxiety was significantly impairing my ability to function.

Not all anxiety is healthy and it's important to recognize where your anxiety falls on the healthy / unhealthy continuum.

THE FUNCTION OF SOCIAL ANXIETY IN ASD

So that's how anxiety works in the typical brain. But what about in the autistic brain?

From childhood, autistic people know that we're missing key information in social situations. We often have difficulty interpreting facial expressions, tone of voice, body language, and non-concrete speech. Some people also struggle with auditory processing and sensory overload in public or group settings.

The results of our social communication challenges can range from inconvenient (missing a joke or not following a conversation) to dangerous (being bullied, taken advantage of, or assaulted). There are also negative health consequences—many autistic people need hours or days to physically recover from prolonged or intense social interaction.

Over time, "through the process of anxiety induction," we realize that certain social situations are "environmental hazards that must be avoided" (as Romanczyk and Gillis described). In other words, because of a very real hazard, we develop anxiety that for us has a very real cause. It isn't disordered. It's a defense mechanism, developed through "the association of certain stimuli with unpleasant consequences."

Social anxiety is not only "important for adaptive functioning" in autistic people, it's essential.

Autistic social anxiety is not the same as neurotypical social anxiety. If a person with intact social communication abilities has severe anxiety about social situations, then they have a disorder because their fear is irrational. They are anxious about doing something that they are capable of doing. When a person with impaired social communication abilities has anxiety about social situations, they are like a poor swimmer who is anxious about boarding a boat. The perceived risk is real and rational.

If fear is a red light—a glowing stop signal in our brain—then anxiety is a yellow light. It's the feeling that says, "Caution, slow down, pause for a moment before continuing down this road."

We should heed this feeling, not cure ourselves of it.

APPROPRIATE VS. INAPPROPRIATE

But, some will say, too much social anxiety and you'll become a recluse. A hermit. The little old lady shouting at those darn kids to get off her lawn.

Well, yes and no. To me, people aren't all that interesting and the rewards of socializing are sometimes overrated. Consider the possibility that the following (fictional) people are meeting their needs for social interaction:

- the person who lives alone, works at home, and in the evening participates in role-playing games, an acting workshop, and a drumming circle
- the nonworking person who lives with a partner and has lunch once a week with a close friend
- the person who attends classes full time and prefers to socialize online in text-based formats outside of class hours
- the person who chooses to spend time at home with family and only goes out for necessary errands or events
- the person who works with people all day and likes to spend their evenings and most of their weekends alone.

The social preferences of these people may differ from the majority of their peers, but they aren't exactly in *Grey Gardens*[2] territory.

Being anxious about socializing is not the same as completely avoiding social situations. It's possible to manage social anxiety in the same way we manage anxiety about other things. Someone—neurotypical or autistic—might feel anxious about starting a new job, but that doesn't mean they

---

2 See, for example, http://greygardensonlines.com.

won't do it. Most people have strategies for managing anxiety and autistic people are no different.

What is different is that autistic social anxiety is automatically pathologized. We're told that our fear is irrational and we need to change the way we think about social interaction. We're told that if we just relax a little we'll find social interaction much more enjoyable.

What would be far more helpful is to acknowledge autistic social anxiety as valid and support autistic people in socializing at their preferred level, in preferred ways.

WHAT ANXIETY TELLS US

So how does social anxiety keep us safe?

First, there is the obvious example: when you have difficulty interpreting nonverbal cues, it can be hard to know when another person is a threat. This can be especially true for autistic women and girls, increasing our chances of becoming the target of sexual assault, sexual abuse, or domestic violence. The autistic woman who feels anxious about dating, intimate relationships, or venturing into unfamiliar situations has good reason to—the statistics for violence against autistic women are alarming.

Autistic people are commonly victims of bullying. The autistic boy or girl who is anxious about recess or the school bus has a large databank of negative interactions feeding that anxiety. Their anxiety tells them that unstructured activities with limited adult supervision are a potential danger zone.

Those are both reasonable examples, right? But what about the anxiety-inducing holiday party, trip to the mall, or vacation? Surely that's irrational?

Not when you have to think about every social activity in terms of cost. Autistic people have limited resources and we need to be aware of how we're spending them.

Last spring my nephew and his wife came to visit for a long weekend. He's one of my favorite nephews and I was looking forward to meeting his new wife. Still, I was anxious. Having two additional people in the house for three days would mean a disrupted schedule, unfamiliar noises and smells, a loss of my precious alone time, and lots and lots of talking.

Sang and I came up with a schedule—scheduling is essential for me to get through three days of company—and then I set about thinking of ways to conserve my resources. I volunteered to drive because I find it relaxing. We scheduled downtime for me on Saturday afternoon while everyone else went out. I suggested we visit a historical site that I knew well, because it would mean a familiar environment plus the chance to infodump in a socially acceptable way.

We had a great time. They enjoyed the places we visited and the meals I cooked. We laughed a lot and had meaningful conversations. Things couldn't have gone better. And still, Saturday night as everyone sat around the dinner table talking for hours after the meal was finished, I found myself shaking uncontrollably.

Even with all of my planning, even though I was enjoying myself, the day's socializing had overwhelmed me. I knew it was coming, had felt myself shutting down as the evening wore on, but I ignored the warning signs. I didn't want to end a great day on a negative note.

Unfortunately, it's not about what I want. Social interaction has a real physical cost. If I don't listen to the voice of caution in my head and limit my interactions, my body will eventually take over and limit them for me.

When I'm in a situation where I feel comfortable, I can handle longer periods of social interaction. When I have to deal with unstructured activities, unfamiliar places, new people, rapid shifts in conversation, partners, or topics, or any of a long list of other things I find challenging, I'll hit my limit sooner. An hour might be all I can deal with before I start feeling a strong need to escape.

Since being diagnosed with Asperger's, I'm getting better at reading myself. The anxiety, the need to escape, and the withdrawal that precedes the uncontrollable shaking are signs that I need to take care—yellow lights to be heeded—and I'm learning to listen to them.

The One Label I'll Never Have

Ninety-eight percent of the time I'm good with being autistic. I was going to say "fine with being autistic" or "okay with being autistic" but I don't want to use tepid adjectives. I really truly feel good about myself most of the time.

Then there's the other two percent. The hard, ugly, maybe I shouldn't be saying this but I'm wishing for normal 2 percent.

When I was four or five years old, I wished I was a boy. Boys got to roughhouse and play cool sports and go shirtless in the summer.

I tried the shirtless thing. It landed me in trouble, though as far as I could tell I looked no different from the shirtless boys in the neighborhood. Later, I hung around the pick-up games and sometimes the older kids let me play. I learned to throw a tight spiral and catch a long pass no matter how bad it made my ice-cold hands sting afterward. Eventually, I learned to fight.

The desire to be a boy faded.

In third grade, I wished my curly hair was straight like Marsha Brady's. All of the cool older girls—and by older I was thinking fifth graders—had straight hair. Somehow, it seemed like straight hair would magically make me popular.

A couple of years later "Farrah Fawcett hair" was all the rage, and if I spent enough time with my mother's blow dryer and roller brush, I could feather my hair perfectly. It didn't make me popular but it cured me of the illusion that better hair was the key to eternal happiness.

I've wished for other things over the years. To be taller (more clothing choices). To be more coordinated (and play high school sports). To be more feminine (I'm not sure why, exactly).

As I've gotten older, the wishes have become more amorphous.

After all of my struggles with new labels in the past year, I find myself trying to sort out where this wishing to be normal falls. Is it like wishing for Marsha Brady hair—that one elusive change that will make me fit in? Or is it like wishing to be a boy so I can play shirtless in the summer?

Surprisingly, I think it's more of the latter—more of a practical wish. I most often find myself wishing to be normal when I see the people around me struggling with the—well, for lack of a better term, let's call it the side effects of my autism.

I don't live in a vacuum. I say and do stuff. People around me are affected by it. Even though they know I struggle with certain things, they know it logically. That doesn't prevent them from being emotionally affected by my words or actions or lack of words or actions.

This is when the wish to be normal sneaks up and grabs me.

I'm using normal and not neurotypical here for a reason. Normal is an illusion and I know it's the illusion that I'm wishing for at these times. I'm not wishing for a different neurology so much as a fantasy version of life.

It's easy to be seduced by the idea that being normal would solve everything, that it would make the lives of the people around me easier. But of course it wouldn't. We'd have some other problems instead, because life is like that.

And that's been a lesson I've learned countless times over this past year: the importance of perspective. The economist Fabian Linden said, "It is useful occasionally to look at the past to gain a perspective on the present" but I think the opposite is also true. By looking at the present, I've also been able to gain a perspective on my past.

13

Arriving at Acceptance

I've lost count of how many times I've seen *The Sound of Music*. It first aired on television when I was seven. Soon after that, it became an annual event, usually running on a Sunday night sometime in January if my memories are correct. As soon as the new year rolled around, I would start checking the TV Guide listings, anxious to discover the exact day of that year's airing. In an era before video on demand—or even video cassettes—the only way to see your favorite movie was to schedule your life around the precious few hours that the networks decided to air it.

As a kid, I thought *The Sound of Music* was a movie about a big family of kids who liked to sing and play tricks on their governesses. I liked the songs and how Maria made their play-clothes out of drapery. The World War II storyline sailed right over my head. The years passed and slowly it dawned on me that this wasn't a movie about a bunch of little kids. No, it was about a teenage girl's tragic first love and a confused young woman who would never be a nun.

Still more years passed and my view of the movie changed again. By then I was an adult with a DVD player, subjecting my family to our own "very special broadcasts" of the movie over Christmas holiday breaks. And now it was a classic love story—a man and woman who are destined to be together against all odds.

The thing is—*The Sound of Music* never changed. It's the same movie today that it was back in 1976. What did change was me. The way I related to the movie, the parts that I zeroed in on, and the parts I overlooked changed as my understanding of life and my experiences grew over the years.

Learning that I'm autistic has been a lot like realizing that *The Sound of Music* is actually a movie about family and romance and war and finding your true calling. Just like the movie, what I am hasn't changed but how I see myself has. My diagnosis has given me context for understanding myself in ways I hadn't thought possible.

That's not to say that my Asperger's diagnosis magically fixed everything. Being on the spectrum still creates day-to-day challenges. Life is often difficult in the same ways it was difficult before. The big difference is that now I have a better understanding of *why* it's difficult. That knowledge has allowed me to begin writing about things beyond my original question of "What does it mean to be autistic?" More and more, I'm confronting the fundamental questions of "What does it mean to be me?"

In a way, they are the same question. There are aspects of me that are clearly autistic. I wouldn't stim so much if I wasn't autistic. I wouldn't have the same sensory sensitivities or communication difficulties. The way I experience my body and the world around me would be very different. But not everything is so clear cut.

Low self-esteem. Anxiety. Perfectionism. Risk taking. Outside the box thinking. Difficulty identifying my needs and wants. Would these aspects of me be the same if I wasn't autistic? How does being on the spectrum interact with my innate personality to make me who I am?

These all feel like questions for the future.

Blogging about my discoveries as I researched autism has been invaluable. Writing helps me process my experiences in a way that is different from thinking or talking about them. It forces me to be with my feelings and to organize my thoughts so they make sense to others, which of course means that by the time I'm done, they make sense to me as well. Essentially, I've been writing the articles that I want to read.

My knowledge of autism has created a foundation for understanding aspects of myself that I've always found frustrating and at times have been ashamed of. It's helped me to struggle less with myself, which has led to struggling less with life. It's been a source of comfort in my relationships, helping me move away from self-judgment toward an attitude of "How can I make this work?"

Understanding my autistic nature takes away a lot of the guesswork in life. Not only have I learned why I do things, I've benefited from the insights of the other autistic adults who comment on what I write. Each new post brings with it opinions, corrections, agreement, and disagreement. When I look back at the first few months of my writing, I have to laugh at how sure of myself I sounded. The input of others has taught me that my experience of Asperger's is uniquely my own.

Autistic people share many traits in common, but it truly is a spectrum. While we have broadly similar experiences, the details of those experiences can be as different as night and day. Yes, most of us have sensory sensitivities, but no one else experiences the exact combination of sensitivities that I do. Yes, we all stim, but everyone's set of stims is unique. For every commenter who responds to a post with an emphatic "this!" there will be someone who says their experience has been very different.

Often it's said that autistic people have difficulty with perspective taking and blogging has been a great lesson in seeing the world through other people's eyes.

It's also been a lesson in compassion.

I went into blogging thinking I would write stuff and maybe people would read it and maybe they would like it and I didn't think past that. I never anticipated how many people would share their own stories in response to what I wrote. Initially, this scared me. I had no idea how to respond. I've never been an especially sympathetic person. A combination of emotional self-protection and difficulty with putting myself in another person's shoes has always made it hard for me to share another person's pain.

But there I was, suddenly confronted with difficult comments and ill equipped to reply. From the small amount of writing I'd shared on the blog at that point, I knew how hard it was to write about painful experiences. In that feeling, I found a "way in." I also saw that in each story there was something I could relate to, some shared experience around which I could build a response. I was struck by the possibility that my difficulty with empathizing wasn't rooted in a defective way of seeing the world, but in a lack of common ground. I've always done my best to intellectually understand what others are feeling, but to truly feel what they were feeling was challenging. Until now.

Slowly, with practice, I learned to receive each comment with an open mind and an open heart. From there, I was able to respond from a place of compassion to others' sadness and anger and loneliness and fear. And as I did, I found myself accessing my own experiences of those feelings.

Maybe compassion for others was a prerequisite to allowing myself to open up those painful dark places inside. In the process of learning to be gentle with others, I'd laid the foundation to being gentle with myself, the foundation for liking myself.

The most important thing I've learned since my diagnosis, by far, has been acceptance. I'd spent a lifetime trying to figure out what was wrong with me. It was as if I'd been looking at myself in a funhouse mirror, seeing a distorted reflection. No matter how I transformed myself, the "me" I saw in the mirror still looked somehow wrong. It was only after learning that I'm autistic that I realized the mirror itself was broken.

I no longer compare myself to what I saw in that funhouse mirror. Instead, I'm learning to look inward, to see myself unfiltered, as I am, as I always have been.

Index